Accidental Traveller

Raphael Wilkins

Grosvenor House
Publishing Limited

This book is published by
Grosvenor House Publishing Ltd
28-30 High Street, Guildford, Surrey, GU1 3EL.
www.grosvenorhousepublishing.co.uk

A CIP record for this book
is available from the British Library

ISBN 978-1-78623-032-4

Contents

Chapter One

I shelter from a tropical downpour: a middle-aged man on my own, a long way from home. The rhythm of beating rain slows, then stops as if someone has turned off the tap. Weak sunlight illuminates Raffles' statue. The harbour is edged with a row of tethered, rocking, rain-bespattered boats of similar local design. On either side of their prows they are painted with a black and white eye, inside a green rhombus edged with red and white. They each bear a number and are offering trips. Memories of boyhood with Grandpa: no seaside holiday complete without a boat ride. Why not? I am out of sight of anyone who might tell me not to. Today I am a tourist. In response to a hailed invitation from Number SC108F, I step along a slender, wet wooden jetty and down into the vessel.

It is a broad clinker-built motorboat with an open well, covered with a canopy whose edges are flapping. I walk down the port side to the passenger area aft, where there are wooden slatted seats with backs, facing forward. Amidships is a wooden construction like a crate on which there is a sound system. The gangway to the starboard side of this is closed off with more slats, to create a separate 'staff' area forward. The canopy rests on curved wooden rafters, from which hang orange-shaded Chinese lanterns. On the first leg of the trip, across the harbour towards a multi-colour patchwork of eating-places lining the other shore, I am the only passenger. A few more board from a wooden jetty, the twin of the one I had used.

The tour begins by heading upstream into the city, past moored craft and under bridges gaily decorated, perhaps for a festival. Various sights are pointed out by the boatman through a scratchy loudspeaker. Then back downstream to the main harbour area, heading towards the sea. Sights include the old post-office, skyscrapers, a few traces of the old town which survived its transformation. A metal sculpture depicts a group of children leaping gleefully from the pavement into the water. The boat chugs out of the mouth of the harbour. Now bright sun lights up the lion statue, of white stone with a jet of water pouring from its mouth, and the boat turns to offer the full panorama of the waterfront prospect. Impressive enough: a prospect of wealth, enterprise and achievement, from central business district, to Ferris wheel and multi-coloured stadium, and forests of dock cranes beyond, but actually it is the water which takes my breath away. Limpid, silky, tropical, multi-coloured: turquoise, lilac, indigo and amber – illuminated, glittering. Startled, I remember a dream.

In my young adulthood I was going nowhere in real life, and perhaps as compensation, I dreamt of embarking on exciting expeditions, only to find that at a vital checkpoint I lacked ticket, passport or some other essential. In one such dream, by some unspecified reckless, illicit act, I found myself on a ship in tropical waters, as dawn broke. From a porthole I gorged my eyes on calm tropical sea, thinking that it was worth whatever recompense would be exacted for this experience. The water was bright, vivid and exquisitely coloured: my dreaming self knew nothing from real life on which to base this image, only a yearning imagination. That dream never recurred, but thirty years later as the boat turned round, up from the depths that imagined image came to call 'snap' to its real counterpart. The clean-edged skyscrapers of Singapore rose proudly, floating on their ripplely-edged reflections, and a voice in my head said, 'So, you see, you've made it at last.'

Chapter Two

It is springtime in Bloomsbury in the year 2007. Bloomsbury has beneficial qualities as a work-place. Just as mineral-infused spa water aids the joints, so a century and a half of literary, artistic and philosophical conversations have infused the fabric of the buildings, and as I walk around, this essence wafts out and aids my mind. I haven't noticed any effect yet, but these things take time.

I am an educationist: a great field to work in because you avoid the bother of having to leave school, enter adult life and find a real job. You just stay on, but with enhanced status as a sort of senior prefect with privileges, such as being allowed to leave the school site and not having to take part in PE.

From my Bloomsbury base, I work mainly in London. I don't get to travel abroad as part of my work. It is a known fact that in order to be allowed to do international consultancy, you must already have a track record of international consultancy. How those in the business got their first assignment is something polite people don't ask about. I do actually do a kind of international work, because foreign delegations come here and I talk to them. I have been doing that recently: a group from India, organised by the British Council. They are linked with a similar group in England.

I am not an afternoon person. I wonder if I might be more productive going out to a tea-room. Or perhaps have an early finish in order (I only partially convince myself) to get a better working evening. The phone rings. I rouse myself enough to remember my name and to show an interest if someone wants to buy something.

It is Susie from the British Council, a very nice young woman. She is thanking me for contributing to the seminar. How polite to take the trouble to make a thank-you call! Perhaps she writes letters after Christmas. 'So now you've been part of the UK end, would you like to see the India end of the project?' This wakes me up: did I hear that correctly? I burble and stammer in an attempt to seek clarification. Is this a hypothetical question about my likes, or a proposition? And if the latter: what, why, how, when and with whose money? Calmly Susie invites me to speak at a seminar in Delhi, at British Council expense, and offers to set up some school visiting to make the trip worthwhile, and to pay a daily allowance, and to make all the arrangements, and to have me escorted everywhere, and make it all OK. My head reels, my palms sweat and I express my grateful acceptance.

Putting down the phone, I, for whom an afternoon in Calais would be an enormous scary adventure, absorb

how my life has been suddenly and unexpectedly transformed. I am going to India! This is what it must be like
to be told you have won the lottery. Nothing will be the
same again. Who can I tell? I spend the next half-hour
wandering around in a daze, finding people to whom
I can announce excitedly, 'I am going to India!' Soon the
daunting practicalities take centre stage: travel clinic,
luggage, camera, half a chemist's shop. Old India hands
advise me. Meanwhile Susie organises everything to do
with the visa and flights, which is just as well as I last
flew before the era of electronic tickets.

I love Stanfords, the map and guide-book shop in
Covent Garden for real travellers. Now I had legitimate
business loitering there, among grizzled yachtsmen
buying nautical charts, and people who look as if they
have hitch-hiked from Vladivostock and are now
browsing large scale maps of Greenland. I buy a guide-
book to India, and a map of Delhi and place them
proudly on the counter: *yes look at me, I need these,
because I am going to India.*

After landing, headachy, leg-achy, I disembarked, following the crowds like a lost soul, scared of going the
wrong way, getting lost in the terminal or doing something wrong. I wanted to get to the safe space of a hotel
room. It was good to know that the British Council
would be meeting me. I visualised a gentleman in a
morning suit with a white carnation, a strip of red
carpet perhaps, and a team of people to care for my
luggage and comforts. Through immigration at last, and
with great relief reunited with my suitcase, I bought
some rupees and approached the exit. I was not yet used
to Asian airports in which people meeting an arrival are

not allowed inside, so I was beginning to get anxious. Then I saw a recognisable approximation of my name on a square of cardboard held by a smiling gentleman: the driver sent by the hotel.

As he led me towards the car a blast of heat hit my face, and crowds of people shouted and jostled around me in a manic competition with each other to sell me things, or carry luggage, or take me to a taxi, or whatever else their cacophony might have meant. Safely in the air-conditioned car, the driver offered me water, which I refused, not trusting its source or my bladder capacity. Then he started giving me a smooth running commentary of passing sights, in a thick accent I could hardly understand. This I found rather uncomfortable. I just wanted to get to the hotel. What do you say apart from 'mm', 'yes', 'I see'? Sometimes he asked, 'Are you liking my commentary?' This made me more uncomfortable because I thought he might expect payment for the service rendered. But I had to be polite. I couldn't say, 'No, I don't need to know the names of these places, or to crick my neck straining to look at things I can't see anyway. I just want to get to the hotel.' He threatened to give me a guided tour: I didn't know whether he meant on a future occasion, or now. Presumably for money. 'I just want to get to the hotel', I said.

Eventually, mercifully, the driver passed me into the attentive, fussy, caring hands of doormen at The Claridges Hotel. This was located in quite a central position within New Delhi, by a roundabout midway between India Gate and the Diplomatic Enclave: an ambience of spacious, leafy, low density development. I was guided down a long, dimly lit but very shiny

7

corridor. The doors and other woodwork were shiny white gloss; the floor was shiny parquet of mainly pale wood, inset with dark stripes each side like 'no parking' lines, and dark diamonds in various patterns. A row of lights along the centre of the ceiling was reflected in the floor, and set other surfaces glinting. The ample room had a large bed with a stack of pillows and scatter cushions, and a balcony looking out over the hotel's front garden. This offered a prospect of tall palm trees, other trees, something that looked like banana bushes, neatly clipped hedges in immaculate borders, perfectly manicured green velvet lawns, and dazzling white chairs, tables and gazebos.

My schedule allowed just enough time for a late lunch, which I selected from the à la carte menu in the hotel's dining room. As a keen frequenter of Indian restaurants, I was aware several times of reminding myself, 'This is not an Indian restaurant in London: this is the real thing.' At 15.45 a car came to take me the short distance to the British Council, which was located inside the British Embassy in the Diplomatic Enclave.

I continued to harbour illusions. When I saw scheduled a meeting at the British Council, I thought 'how nice!' and imagined a version of tea at the vicarage, only much posher. It would be in a building like a small stately home, with fine china, and aristocratic Englishmen putting me at my ease whilst in a foreign country, saying things like, 'Jolly good: drop in any time, we're always here to help you.' By contrast, the way in to the concrete building was like passing through the guard room of a high-security barracks, all entrants being treated as if they were suspected of being dangerous asylum-seekers.

Once inside, I waited in a busy foyer, where the main activity seemed to be selling courses in English for speakers of other languages. My meeting was with two Indian members of staff working on the project with which I was involved: it was just a normal, unmemorable work meeting.

That evening was, however, memorable. Showing more courage than for a long time before or since, I decided to go out, while it was still light, on my own, to explore the Lodi Gardens. A colleague had mentioned that this was a pleasant spot. Getting back to the hotel at about 17.15, I quickly exchanged my blue business suit for a cream summer jacket, and, map in hand, stepped out into India.

Two things interested me about the roundabout. First, the range of traffic going round it, which included ordinary modern vehicles; swaying, elderly-looking lorries of a notably 'foreign' design; motorised rickshaws with yellow hoods and green bodies, open at the side; and motor bikes and scooters, usually carrying two or more people. Secondly, the style of driving: those entering the roundabout did so into the path of the traffic circulating, rather than giving the circulating traffic priority in the European manner. This worked fine, because drivers drove slowly, caringly, and, as I later discovered, were used to avoiding cows wandering into the road.

I crossed Aurangzeb Road and took South End Road, crossing two further roads to reach the gardens. I was interested to feel the heat of the air, as a pleasurable new experience. The road was tree-lined, and spacious, with a strip of grass between pavement and road: it felt safe.

I wondered what happened about the fruit growing in these public places: could anyone eat the mangoes?

At the entrance to the Lodi Gardens, painted metal signs in Hindi and English explained the restricted hours during which dogs on leashes were allowed, how opening hours varied between seasons, and various rules. The sun was starting to set as I walked between tall palms to the first of many 15th Century tombs of sultans. These were mostly of a reddish tinge, with the mortar in fact being redder than the stones. All of the monuments were huge, ornate, astonishingly old, and were simply *there*, completely accessible for people to enjoy.

A peacock strutted along in front of a tall castellated structure. Later, I came to the massive, highly decorated, honey-coloured structure which is the Bara Gumbad with attached mosque, built in 1494. Square and domed, it sat on a lawn in a public park: I could not believe that such important antiquities were not guarded in some way. A painted board showed pictures of birds, with the names and descriptions unfortunately only in Hindi. Some were the same or similar to those in Europe; others more exotic. Light was fading as I crossed over some stinking stagnant water, passed a tree with leaves of flaming red, and joined a sparse procession of family groups heading towards the exit.

At one level, I was just taking a walk in a park, but all the while, I was experiencing what I can only describe as some kind of spectator syndrome, so self-conscious was my sense of doing something that I regarded as pro-foundly significant. I retraced my route, savouring my first taste of velvet hot-country night, and felt a wave of relief and accomplishment when I was back inside the hotel.

Next morning, Tuesday 1 May, I explored the excitements of the breakfast buffet, discovering the wonderful refreshing qualities of watermelon juice. My selection of foods was adventurous because I felt sure that the opportunity would not arise again: it included idli rice dumplings with hot sambhar. At 9.30 a car came to take me to the Blue Bells International School, for some educational tourism.

During the drive, I drank in the street scene. In a typical view, near to the school, the road was separated by a surface of varying materials from a line of buildings several storeys high, penetrated by alleys and clearly extending back some way. These buildings were a jumble of styles, purposes and ages. A modern shop frontage announced 'Cheese Bazaar: known for its quality'; next door, a printed fabric sign stuck on the wall above what looked like a metal garage door advertised motor repairs by a consultant engineer with a lot of qualifications. Across an alley, tumbledown shacks offered vaguely described services such as 'Shish Enterprises'. On the ground between the building line and the road, modern cars were parked. Between these, a man was selling something in jars, on a stall set up on what looked like a perambulator, standing in the full glare of the sun. Some sort of street food vending stall was shaded by an umbrella. Bicycles were propped here and there. An ancient wooden handcart stood empty. Scrawny hump-backed cows wandered freely among these objects. A group of men sat in a line, passing the time in conversation.

I was worried about how I would cope physically with the day, being prone to headaches and upset stomachs: both exacerbated by stress such as travel, unusual food and environments, meeting new people, and having to be on my best behaviour. The school was an elite independent school for girls, guided by 'a global vision of the world being one family', and a curriculum 'highlighting universal peace and brotherhood', and clearly accustomed to offering a smoothly polished visitor experience.

After introductions, I was shown a film about the school, then allocated one of the senior staff as guide. Back through the foyer, covered with high quality displays illustrating the school's ethos and achievements, the tour began in the grounds. I saw a garden dedicated to engineering and technological innovation, containing various pieces of interactive equipment, in addition to the more usual facilities for formal and informal recreation. The lawns and flower borders were immaculate. A small army of, presumably, lower caste workers grubbed at them on their hands and knees. Delhi was beginning one of its hottest summers for a while, and after seeing these sights in the full sun, bare-headed and wearing a business suit, I was pleased to get back inside. There, I was taken on the usual kind of tour, followed by lunch in a separate staff room set up especially for the occasion.

My lunch companions were six or seven women in middle or senior management positions, elderly and serious, but determined to be hospitable. I was hungry but surveyed the meatless spread dejectedly. Among the tediously long list of foods I have to avoid are citrus fruits (and their juices used in cooking) and cheese, which are migraine triggers, and I have to be careful with dairy products generally as they can be upsetting. Before me was an oily curry of paneer (lumps of cottage cheese), a bowl of curds, a bowl of yoghurt, and a plate with cubes of cheddar-style cheese. There must also have been some rice or bread, I can't remember.

The women ate little, but supervised me fussily, obviously taking it for granted that I would find everything scrumptious. 'Please permit me the honour of placing some of *these* onto your plate', said one, adding to my troubles. After lunch, I was granted a brief audience with the founder-proprietor, a formidable personage who glared at me as if I had crawled out of a hole. A scarf of golden satin, bearing the school's badge, was placed on me in the manner of a clergyman's stole, and a group photograph was taken.

Back at the hotel, I laid on the bed with a cold wet flannel over my face until it was time to change into a clean shirt and go out for the next engagement. At 16.00 the car came for me. Susie was in the back: it was nice to see her. We were going to visit Professor Marmar to plan Thursday's seminar. I had met Professor Marmar in London: he was small, animated, learned, opinionated and very talkative in quite a friendly way. He was important: not just in his own estimation, but in having been recommended to the project by an Indian expert of global status. He had various affiliations, and on his business card he was the Director of an educational technology and management academy, so I assumed the meeting would be in a work setting.

The driver had trouble finding the place and had to keep stopping to ask for directions. Eventually he deposited us near to a heavy, dented, buckled metal door of the kind that might protect an electrical sub-station or an ammunition store. Marmar shoved it ajar and invited us to step through onto the cement floor of a modestly furnished sitting room. Here, while my head pounded, we had our discussion. Marmar went and got us tea and a light snack, which included cucumber raita and cakes. On the way back to the hotel, Sarah told me that Tim was arriving that evening and would accompany me the following day. Tim was a headteacher of a UK school involved in the project. He had an Indian wife, had spent long periods in India, and was proficient in Hindi and Urdu: a most reassuring companion.

That evening I browsed the hotel's small shopping arcade. I knew that this would be an expensive place to buy things, but it was convenient. In the men's outfitters I bought a mandarin-style jacket in black and gold brocade, a black silk shirt without collar, and a patterned silk shirt in brilliant blue. Next door, there were some carpets. I have been buying oriental rugs for decades and am less gullible than the average tourist. I was, nevertheless, persuaded to buy a small mat for about the same price I would have paid for it in Durham. I had not rehearsed emphasising one purchase only, so after that I was persuaded into buying a hand embroidered tablecloth and set of serviettes. It was nice work, slaved over by someone, and quite expensive. When I got home, it went into a sideboard cupboard, and has not been out since.

As night follows day, my stomach became upset. In addition to all the normal factors, on one occasion of forgetfulness I had started brushing my teeth with tap water, which may have added to the features and duration of my indisposition. The people who serviced the room did slightly odd things in their fussy way. They liked to lay the mat for standing on when you get out of the bath in front of the toilet: why would I want it there? Whenever I went out, I would leave a wet face flannel ready to cool my fevered brow when I returned. It was always replaced by a hot dry one.

Wednesday's expedition was to a school just over an hour and a half's drive to the north-west of Delhi. It was a Government-provided boarding school intended to benefit talented girls from poor rural families. We understood that term had already finished, so expected our meeting to be just with the headteacher. Tim was a mine of information throughout the day.

The drive started in the busy streets of Delhi. Ahead of us I saw lorries, buses, cars, a fuel tanker, several vehicles abreast and churning clouds of dust and exhaust fumes. Between these heavy vehicles, motorbikes carried couples and families, the women sitting side saddle, with cerise or primrose chiffon garments flowing in the breeze, maintaining their balance through the din, dust and swerving hazards.

As we approached the edge of the city, the traffic thinned and became more varied. A confusing and colourful variety of small shops lined the road, which was also edged with street-selling enterprises of different kinds. Between these, and to some extent almost amongst them, moved rickshaws for goods and passengers, handcarts, motorbikes and bicycles, and cows.

Vehicles threaded their way through, straying over into the opposite lane as necessary.

On a modern stretch of road like a motorway, I saw traffic lights with a count-down display: these did not appear in London until a few years later. At these stopping points, sweltering and mainly very dark-skinned street vendors would move among the vehicles offering prepared portions of coconut, and other goods. A woman came to the window of our car: she was not carrying any goods, but persistently rapped on the glass, pointing to me and then to herself, smiling.

We passed through a couple of small towns or large villages, and I longed to understand what actually happens in them: how the economy operates, how daily life proceeds. What I saw was a street scene similar to that described earlier, but more spaced out and more dilapidated, with piles of rubble and buildings which seemed partially fallen down. Ancient workshops were full of dusty, rusty vintage bikes and motorbikes of the kind a museum would love. Shops, patches of rough ground that looked like scrap yards, groups of leaning telegraph poles, rickety street-café style chairs and tables – all looked as if they had not been touched for a long time. Amongst all this, many people, mainly men, sat in groups, or stood motionless, apparently doing nothing at all. It was as if a bomb had hit the place 50 years ago and everyone was still too stunned to think about making a start on clearing up the mess.

Vehicles took wide detours from their lane to avoid potholes. A camel-drawn cart carried an enormous wide load of bales, probably of hay or straw. In the countryside I saw simple buildings abutted by neat stacks of sun-dried dung patties, and neat stacks of dung not made into patties. In fact dung was quite a feature of the landscape. The landscape itself, disregarding the heat, was surprisingly universal. I saw vistas of golden cereal fields dotted with dark green trees, some patches of bright green crops, areas of rough pasture and scrub: scenes which could have been painted by Constable or by French Impressionists.

The driver stopped several times to ask for directions. Tim explained to me quietly that people don't like to disappoint, so tend to say 'yes' to questions phrased in the form, 'Is it this way?' Eventually the driver took us into the drive leading to the school. We were surprised to see some students playing in the grounds. As we approached the headquarters building, Tim said 'We have a reception committee'. A line of students stood with the headteacher outside the front door. Letting Tim go first, and following his example as to protocol, we bent our heads in front of a student with a small brass dish of red paste, who fingered a patch of it onto our foreheads. We bent again in front of another student, each to have placed over our head a garland of fragrant rose blossoms.

Thus honoured, we were invited by the headteacher, a mature man of military bearing, to his office. He offered coffee. I asked for black tea, which would have been very welcome. 'Chai!' he countermanded, believing that to be superior, and in due course the servant reappeared with the sweet, boiled-up milky confection that forms a thick skin. After that I asked to use the toilet, which was a hole in the ground. The headteacher took us on a tour of the school. It was empty except for token groups of students, amounting perhaps to two or three classes. We were taken to watch a lesson on business studies. Using a scuffed blackboard covered in barely legible writing, a teacher explained some aspect of accounting to the small class, occupying a fraction of the room's ancient wooden desks. Then we saw some feature, such as a computer room, and a few minutes later went to another room, by which time we were able to see the same group of students having an equally artificial science lesson. We saw the library in which we were able to meet a unit of uniformed cadets, some of whom had been sitting in the lessons.

We had a tour of the site, including a great open-sided barn which was the cooking and eating area. Vicious looking insects hovered about. We went as far as the vestibule in one of the dormitory blocks. A highlight was a display of arts and crafts, mainly set up in an external area shaded by trees. There were practical demonstrations of hand-painting, chalk-making, sand-painting, candle-making, lino printing, ceramics, and many more things. Although term had ended, the head-teacher had required these classes to stay behind for some days, in order to mount this full-scale open day exhibition, purely for our benefit. He invited us to have lunch in his house.

Over rice, curds and a hot, watery, vegetable curry, the headteacher spoke hospitably, mainly about military matters and politics, and his judgements regarding the qualities and limitations of the different ethnic groups that make up India. Afterwards, he took us to a barn-like hall for the finale: to watch some dance routines.

Students sat on the floor; behind them was a row of chairs for adults. From this vantage point, Tim surveyed the backs of heads and said quietly to me, 'You can tell from the proportion of Western hairstyles that most of these girls are not from poor rural families.'

Music played. For a long time I assumed it was recorded, then eventually I worked out that it was a live performance by a group at the edge of the stage, which included some kind of bellows-operated instrument. Groups of girls danced a sequence of traditional dances in various costumes. It was hot, I was tired, it was tedious. My attention wandered, my eyelids drooped. Someone was making a speech. Through semi-consciousness, I was alarmed to hear the words, 'And now it is my honour to invite Professor Wilkins to the platform to address us.' 'Professor' was a purely honorary title conferred on me by the speaker. Why had I not anticipated this? Why had I not been using the last hours of drudgery to compose some uplifting oratory? Why had the headteacher not given me some warning? I was the opposite of a natural impromptu speaker. My expression must have been one of shock and dread as I took the long walk to the platform, where I struggled to string together some pedestrian sentences. Then it was Tim's turn: as an experienced headteacher, he was relaxed and in his element; he more than compensated for my deficiencies.

That evening, Tim, Susie and I were driven to the event venue for a drinks reception and dinner. It was in the Atrium Hotel in Faridabad, about an hour's drive to the south of Delhi. It was light for most of the outward journey. We passed tracts of waste ground. Some were littered with objects; some may have been used as camp-sites by homeless people, having low tent-like structures made crudely out of bits and pieces. I enjoyed the buffet meal at the venue, which included some good biryanis, but I was disappointed to find wherever lamb appeared, it came with awkward sharp bones.

On Thursday, the three of us set off at 7.00 for the drive to the venue. We passed a wooded area where there were monkeys in the trees. The car park at the venue was outside, and as the day got hotter I wondered just how hot the cars became. Various activities and presentations occurred, including my own small contribution. I enjoyed browsing the buffet lunch, knowing now to pick around the knobbly pieces of bone. At the end of the day, Tim offered to show us 'the real Delhi' that evening. After a brief stop at the hotel, Tim, Susie, a senior British Council official called Judith, and I, took a taxi to a shopping district. Tim pointed out a government store as a potential source of gifts. It offered the full range of Indian crafts but was quite expensive. In the window was what I took to be a wall hanging. It was in the style of an oriental rug, but was a thick, chunky embroidery made out of what looked like threads of gold and silver among coloured silks.

Outside the shop, a group of young men were operating a press for making juice from sugar canes. A young boy kept pestering me for money, good-naturedly but he was hard to shake off. I had no low-denomination notes. I had become separated from the others and was anxious to catch them up. Tim wanted to show us a market which involved crossing a busy multi-lane road. There were no crossings. Tim instructed us in the Indian method of road crossing. Then he said 'Now!' and the four of us stepped out in a steady, unhurried way, directly into the path of the traffic, and kept walking steadily forward, ignoring the hooting and swerving going on around us. We arrived safely at the other side. It was now dark. We entered a crowded market area. Many of the traders were sitting or squatting in groups on the ground, burning spills of paper to provide light. It was eerie and did not feel like a safe environment: I made sure I stayed near to the others as we progressed along a row of kiosks. Susie took a while sampling perfumes.

It was time to eat. Tim chose a restaurant offering South Indian cuisine, and gave us a tutorial on its components and, later, during the meal, on how to eat them. He went to wash his hands, and came back saying 'Don't use the toilet.' He said there was no running water. He had asked the staff if he could wash his hands; they fobbed him off but he had persisted in their language, and reluctantly they had opened a small bottle of water and poured some over his fingers. So all day, these people who do not use toilet paper had been preparing food in a place with no washing facilities.

After the meal, we went to what Tim thought might be a good tea room, but in the event, what I got was a tea bag with chai flavouring in a cup of hot milk. Conversation ranged over educational subjects, and our favourite places in London for eating nice Indian food.

For the journey back, we discussed getting a ride in one of the old Morris Oxford taxis, but when we investigated, it was too late: they were all packed up. The only option was to take a couple of motorised rickshaws. Tim did the negotiation in whichever language the drivers spoke, making them agree that the fare was about a tenth of what they would have charged a group of Westerners. I was delighted that he decided he and Judith would go in the first, and I would have the pleasure of Susie's company in the second. We squeezed in and set off on a wonderfully atmospheric and hair-raising ride. Susie's close company was a definite plus factor. At traffic lights, maimed beggars would come up and stand silently, poking out stumps and withered arms at us. As we got away from the centre, the pace increased. The two drivers were not actually racing each other, but that was the sensation as we swirled around roundabouts and accelerated along dark deserted boulevards. I expressed something of my joy, and Susie said, 'It's alright for you, you have the rail', which was indeed holding me in. She pointed out that she was on the open side, with nothing at all holding her in. 'Swap sides!' I suggested caringly, 'You'll be much better off over here', as I showed with gestures how easily she could slip across me into a better position. This offer was rejected.

On Friday morning I managed to cram my purchases and various official gifts into my already full baggage, and went to the airport. There, I needed to urinate in a stinking public toilet, which had only a row of holes in the ground. I noticed broom handles shoved into plastic bottles as plungers. There was a cistern and chain, and after I had finished, like a well brought up person would, I pulled it. After a few seconds of suspense, a repulsive surge of raw sewage welled out of the holes and chased me to the door.

During the flight home, between frequent visits to the toilet, I had stunning views of the Himalayas. I felt fulfilled. Albeit somewhat briefly, I had engaged in travel to an exotic location: a once in a lifetime experience. But now over and done with, I thought, although the diarrhoea lasted a month.

Chapter Three

Immediately after my return from India, while I was still savouring the experience, collecting photographs from Boots and trying to sort out my body, a development arose concerning some Saudis. A delegation of Saudis had visited the organisation the previous year, just before my arrival. This occurred from time to time: I had met a different Saudi delegation some months previously, and I had something vague in my diary about another one coming shortly. The group in question, different from these others, had been in touch periodically and now wanted to form a consortium to bid for a large contract that was expected to be advertised in a year or so's time. My organisation judged these talks worth pursuing. In my first week back in the office, I was exchanging e-mails on the matter. The leader of the group, Abdulaziz, said we would need to show our faces in Riyadh. Humphrey in our international unit had a fund to cover business development trips; he got the idea approved, and to my surprise invited me to go with him.

I was completely naïve about the complexity of the procedure for getting a visa to enter Saudi Arabia. The timeline for this affected the scheduling of the trip, and after the hotel and flight bookings had been made, there was uncertainty, right up to the afternoon before travel, about whether the visas would be issued in time.

With keenness which exceeded capability, I had been studying Arabic. I do not have much aptitude for learning languages, and left school with no passes in that field, but every decade or so I suffer a compulsion, always futile, to make an effort to do so. The previous summer, when I had started interacting with Arabic-speaking delegations, the beautiful calligraphy of the script bewitched me, and for courtesy I wanted to master some very basic greetings. Arabic culture seemed exotic and attractive. So I struggled with *Teach Yourself Arabic* and similar texts, and convinced myself as usual that if I invested in texts and placed them near to me, an osmotic process would occur. I also bought a guide to Arabic social customs which turned out to be helpful.

An opportunity to practise my beginner's phrases arose in the form of a visiting delegation. The pencil jotting in my diary firmed into a session on Friday 25 May. I waited in the foyer to meet the group. Ten of them got out of a minibus, with their interpreter. Some delegations present an image designed to impress; others like this one are understated. They were away from their context, in a rag-bag of Western clothes, and seemed relaxed, in a way that belied their statuses as a Deputy Minister and a group of Regional Directors of Education. I escorted them to a similarly downbeat meeting room and tried to discern what they wanted.

When the brief is very vague, it is hard to know whether to give a lecture about the UK education system, or to launch straight into a sales pitch. On this occasion I chose a mixture of the two.

Meanwhile, Abdulaziz was demonstrating the smooth efficiency of the Arab trader. He was a former Minister, who had developed an attachment with a major Saudi corporation which specialised in training technical personnel. Now he needed to add a source of UK educational expertise as the essential third leg of the tripod. To that end, on Wednesday 13 June I found myself in a meeting with my organisation's senior management in London, having a video conference with Abdulaziz and his associates in Riyadh, to make the final arrangements for the trip.

We were due to fly on Saturday 16 June. On Thursday afternoon, Humphrey dropped into my office and gave me a plain brown envelope containing a bundle of US Dollars: 'For the trip', he explained vaguely, while bemoaning the uncertainty about whether we would be going or not. At around 16.00 on Friday I got the phone call to say that visas had been issued, and I could collect my passport.

At Heathrow I bought some Saudi Riyals. I understood that, along with the US Dollar, these were one of the very few, perhaps only other, hard currencies left in the world. The flight was with British Midland, direct to Riyadh: it was half empty and uneventful. 'Death to Traffickers!' was the most prominent sign on arrival, as we queued patiently, slowly moving through the rigorous entry formalities.

Selecting the right kind of taxi is a bit of an issue in Saudi Arabia, as the dress code does not distinguish rogues from gentlemen, and the accosting process starts before being able to see the vehicles in question. Emerging from the terminal into a hot, dark evening, we settled on one that seemed OK, and, as the guide book suggested, I discussed in advance the fare for taking us to the Marriott Hotel. Of the currencies about my person, the driver chose Riyals.

Then we were off. The driver, wearing standard Saudi white dishdash and red-chequered head-dress, sat in a seat covered all over with a great thick fleece, and the surface between the steering wheel and the windscreen was similarly bedecked, as if he would have preferred to have been riding a camel. The drive was along a busy motorway: a stream of flashing headlamps against what seemed to be flat, empty terrain. As buildings became more numerous, they presented a random assortment of unregulated trunk-road ribbon-development: industrial and storage premises, motor trades, retail outlets and occasional places for eating or entertainment, all with bright signs and plenty of flood-lighting. The sensation of being on a motorway continued right into the centre of Riyadh, and up to the front door of the Marriott Hotel.

Here, we passed through security screening facilities staffed by armed guards, into the foyer, where our reservations were easily found. This was Saturday night, and we were not on duty until Monday morning. Humphrey had his laptop with him, and went off to his room with the statement, 'I have no desire to leave this hotel'. I shut the door of my own room and appraised the situation. Any hotel bearing the Marriott label will offer some degree of familiar ambience, but I had two initial impressions of differences. First, all the staff and all the guests were men. This complete absence of females gave the place a certain atmosphere which reminded me of staying in a barracks in the days before the Army went mixed. Secondly, the smell. The hotel, and, I later discovered, Riyadh generally, exuded a faint dusty mustiness which I associate with stone surfaces that have been swabbed with a none-too-clean floor-cloth. Of course it is a miracle of engineering that enough water is produced to meet the needs of a major city in the middle of the desert. When I took a bath the water definitely had plenty of other chemical ingredients to pad out the hydrogen and oxygen. Did it come through long pipes, or from deep wells, or from alchemy? How much of it was recycled?

The bedroom window looked out over flat roofs to a mosque in a side street. House sparrows pecked about on the roof: thin, abstemious versions of their English cousins. The amplified call to prayer started with a wail rising both in pitch and volume, like the onset of an 'all clear' siren. It woke me during the night and in the early morning. To satisfy my curiosity I peeped through the curtain: a scattering of people headed to the mosque on each occasion. Bringing books of any kind into Saudi Arabia, including even improving religious works, was officially discouraged. On the top shelf of the wardrobe was a fusty folded prayer mat, but no Koran: a notice said that hotel staff would provide one if necessary. On the desk, a Qibla arrow was fixed to show the direction of Mecca, to assist in-room devotions. It was of some slight help to me in orientating myself to my inadequate street plan.

In contrast to these austere tones, exploring the restaurant buffet was fun. A Middle-Eastern spread in a real Middle-Eastern place! The pork-free range of cold meats was interesting, with nice dips, and at the dessert stage I enjoyed the selection of different kinds of halva. I was worried about the amount of lemon juice in things, but as usual when confronted by a buffet, I felt it right to try to get my money's worth.

I passed the time somehow on Sunday. I did not have a laptop with me: it must have been a mixture of reading and pen-and-paper work, between leisurely meals. After lunch, I thought I should venture out, although the immediate environs did not look particularly inviting. I went to the foyer and walked towards the security checks. People looked at me strangely as I passed through. No-one actually asked 'Where is your car?', but I realised later this question must have been in their minds. There is no public transport: in towns, the car is king, and not even mad Englishmen go for a stroll along a motorway in Riyadh in June.

Moving a few steps away from the hotel door, towards the road, it became clear that the weather was very hot. Shadows were short, and with the heat came the intense, almost blinding, searchlight glare of the sun. I reached the road, and for want of any better plan, turned left beside it. I tried to summon up some sense of being on a holiday jaunt, or at least, of being a traveller enjoying a new location. I tried to soak up the scene: the interesting traffic thundering past; interesting metal railings and sparrows. Distracting me from these interests was the sensation that my thinning hair had melted, my scalp had been burned away, and my exposed brain was roasting. Or, that I still had my skull, but within it my brain was boiling in its surrounding blood in the manner of a pressure cooker. I wondered for how long it was sensible to carry on. Ahead, I could see the pavement broken by a road junction: the entrance to the next group of buildings. That became my goal. I made it, and noted with a sense of achievement that the traffic, railings and sparrows here were no different. As I retraced my steps, forcing myself to walk naturally, not to make a fool of myself by hurrying to shelter, I remembered Humphrey's wise parting words.

There was a shop in the hotel. I thought I should take some small items home with me. All of the Arabian souvenirs, including yashmaks and head-dresses, had 'Made in China' labels. Eventually I picked a couple of crafty bracelets and a poor quality pokerwork box, with a palm tree design and the words, 'King Dom of Saudi Arabia', and, in smaller letters, 'Made in China'. That evening, for a change, I ordered a room service meal, and enjoyed picking items from the 'Arabian Specialities' section of the menu.

On Monday morning we needed to check out. My envelope of dollars was insufficient to settle the bill, so I used my own credit card, which fortunately worked, and some days later returned the dollars untouched to Humphrey's office. I felt that arrangements for liaison were not robust. I had no means of communicating with Abdulaziz; I assumed Humphrey might be so equipped. These demarcations were never put to the test. As soon as we met at reception, one of many identically dressed figures arose from a settee nearby: it was Abdulaziz, greeting us and efficiently taking charge of everything for the rest of the day.

He took us to his scalding hot Mercedes saloon (each hop of the journey was too short to give the air conditioning much of a chance), and showed us some of the spectacular modern architecture of Riyadh. In most places where he stopped, to lead us on a short walk, police appeared immediately to check the car for explosives, requiring him to open bonnet and boot. Sometimes he made shruggy-gesturing, hands in air, smiley remonstrations at this: 'They are British!'

Photography is not allowed in Saudi Arabia if the shot taken includes any Government building, any woman, or any member of the security forces. In practice, that is very near to saying that it is not allowed at all. According to a guide book, citizens are encouraged to throw stones at anyone breaking the rule. This was, I felt sure, my once-only opportunity to see Riyadh, and I got my camera out and asked Abdulaziz for his guidance. He said that it would be OK for me to take photos so long as I was with him. I came to realize that this is how things work in Saudi Arabia. After a few of these building photo-shoot opportunities I began to worry that the camera was getting so hot it might be damaged: the liquid crystal display seemed to be melting.

Between stopping points, we talked about our different countries: Abdulaziz was keen to show his own in a positive light, and seemed sincere in his views. We passed a gleaming, state-of-the-art hospital. 'We started out as a poor nation, with no natural resources, then God gave us oil so that now we can care for our people', he explained. 'But even in the early days before wealth, the tribes round about chose freely to come under the wise and just rule of the House of Saud', he elaborated.

I mentioned some of the limitations to real choice in UK-style democracy. Abdulaziz was a member of the King's Consultative Council: 'That is our form of democracy'. He thought I might have been to Dubai, and seemed pleased to learn that I had not. 'When a man has been to Dubai, he has not been anywhere', he said dismissively.

We came to the corporate headquarters to meet the Saudi end of the planned partnership. Our meeting was on one of the higher floors of the mainly glass sky-scraper. We were ushered in to an executive meeting area, where I was introduced to the President of the company. I was aware of some manoeuvrings and stage management to set up this encounter, but so smoothly was it done that at the time I did not realise what was happening. The President and the two or three colleagues he had with him were in Saudi dress. They stood in a line, and as I exchanged a formal greeting with the President, I noticed that he was tall: taller than me, a quality also evident when we were sitting at the table. A few months later I met him at the Ritz for lunch, where both standing and sitting, he was quite a bit shorter than me. In both of his forms of presenting himself, he was charming and very well informed.

Refreshments happened. I asked for 'Tea with sugar, please' in Arabic, and following the guide to social customs, twisted the glass when I had had sufficient glassfuls. These small accomplishments were appreci-ated. The discussion progressed. Our hosts needed at times to talk among themselves in Arabic, and needed to break for prayers, while Humphrey and I enjoyed the stunning view from the window. Then a Western-style early lunch of filled rolls was served.

Our next engagement was at the Ministry of Education, where we were scheduled to have an audience with the Crown Prince. Abdulaziz drove us to his old stamping ground and parked in the official car-park. We were swept into the building without any formalities. The meeting room was a panelled chamber with a large central table at which a number of officials were sitting. We were put in the guests' position, at the upper end of the right hand side from the head of the table. Servants performed the tea ceremony, and a low hum of conversation took place. I had been briefed that His Royal Highness the Crown Prince had been given personal responsibility for overseeing the project we hoped to discuss. It was contested terrain: apparently Harvard had had an audience on the same matter a few days previously.

Some kind of signal must have been received: the hum of conversation stopped, and a second later two large doors in the panelling burst open. His Royal Highness strode in briskly and sat at the head of the table. His billowing robes had the gold edging of the royal family. He was clean-shaven, with broad open features, light café-au-lait complexion, and small wire-framed spectacles. He combined the aura of the absolute feudal power of his dynasty, with worldly modern intelligence. Formal introductions and some opening pleasantries occurred. Then I had an opportunity briefly to explain the benefits which my organisation could bring to the Kingdom. The Crown Prince was courteous and attentive, and not at all pompous: he could afford to wear his exalted status lightly. The proceedings lasted about twenty minutes. At a signal everyone in the room stood and he made his exit.

As we moved back into the anteroom, Abdulaziz said he would give us a tour of the Ministry. He took us along corridors, into rooms, up staircases. In an equivalent Western prestigious headquarters, most of the staff would have been female, and many would have exhibited that pleasing combination of brains, beauty, breeding, style and energy which serves corporate careers well. Here, all of that was present but like a mirror image, the staff being entirely male. Elegantly dressed in the Saudi style, perfectly manicured, beautifully handsome young men were everywhere, smiling and twinkling with intelligence and eagerness to please.

My organisation had felt a need to take some soundings about Abdulaziz's standing, given that he was now an ex-Minister, but the agencies approached had not produced much. The tour of the office told its own story: without taking the shine off his genuine hospitality, he was a smooth enough operator to have anticipated the question, to which this was now the answer. Not only was he welcomed everywhere, with real warmth, but as word got around that he was in the building, he held court in the corridors among his well-wishers. He knew all the staff, and had a caring, fatherly manner towards them.

Then he said, 'Let me introduce you to my successor'. He took us towards the end of a corridor, and bade us pause while he checked, before beckoning us forward. We went through an anteroom, staffed with more beautiful young men, into a grand office. It was generously proportioned, richly decorated and with fine large furniture. The Minister sat on a kind of throne, and either side of him a young male assistant tended to his words and needs. They sat on footstools, as acolytes: they were not actually waving palm branches to cool their lord and master, but might just as well have been. Of the Minister, I had the impression initially simply of an important white-robed Arab. Abdulaziz was saying something, probably introducing us, and I began my humble obeisance, bowing with clasped hands, explaining what an honour and privilege it was for me to be able to convey in person the greetings and goodwill of my organisation.

'I met you in London!' the Minister exclaimed. And the spell of context and role-playing was broken. I looked at him properly, and yes, this was the same individual who, three weeks previously, had jumped out of a minibus in an open-necked shirt, odd jacket and trousers, and had brought his delegation into a coffee-stained, wobbly-tabled meeting room. He came down from the chair of state, and perched on a settee which he invited me to share, where we had a perfectly normal professional conversation.

For our next and final official duty, Abdulaziz took Humphrey and me to a restaurant. My memories are hazy regarding what time this was: it could have been construed as a very late lunch, or a somewhat early dinner. Sunset happens early in Saudi Arabia, and the scorching glare was frazzling before, and only slightly abated afterwards. The timing of our arrival at the restaurant had to fit conveniently between prayer times, otherwise the door would be locked and we would have to wait. Abdulaziz thought our meetings at the Ministry had gone well: he was in good spirits. The only place to park the car was in direct sunlight, and I wondered how hot it would become by the time we came back. We walked perhaps a hundred yards, enough for my thin-soled shoes to register the egg-frying qualities of the pavement.

The restaurant was The Village, offering an authentic Arab experience, and a long time after the event it occurred to me that this would have been a set-piece stopping-off point for entertaining foreign visitors, a bit like taking visitors to London to Rules for traditional Edwardian British fare. We entered a dark, cool, stone interior space. From here, a waiter led us out of the back of it into a partially roofed, open air dining area. So it was shaded, but the air was thick with the heat of the day. The dining area was divided into a series of bays separated by walls between two and three feet high around three sides. The floor and walls of each bay were covered in oriental rugs, with cushions scattered here and there.

We sat on the floor. This was no problem for Abdulaziz, but in the case of Humphrey and myself it was done somewhat gingerly. My last experience of regularly sitting cross-legged on the floor was in primary school, which was a long time ago. I found that my mature bones and physique could not hold that posture for more than a few seconds. I opted for a legs to one side mode which presented a less pretty version of how the Copenhagen Mermaid sits on her rock. It was still uncomfortable, and I do not like trying to eat off a plate balanced on my lap. These factors definitely limited my dining, both in quantity and level of enjoyment.

Items began to arrive. A teapot and cups were delivered. Abdulaziz poured some tea into a cup and then back into the top of the teapot. This, he explained, was because the tea in the spout would otherwise be insufficiently infused with mint, a large bunch of which was sitting in the pot. I had not had a satisfying cup of tea since breakfast, as the ceremonial variety had been like pale pond-water. This tea was a wonderfully restoring combination of black tea leaves, spearmint leaves and sugar. Although it was sweeter than I would choose, I couldn't get enough of it: I felt it getting into my veins like an elixir. In fact I may, in my desperate need, have breached normal good manners in causing a second pot to be ordered.

With the tea came very good flatbreads in several different varieties. Other dishes arrived. Most of the food was presented in ornate brass dishes, bowls, plates or trays according to its volume and consistency. Serious eating began, as is necessary to cement good cross-cultural relations. To eat from, we each had a china bowl, of the size we might use for soup or pudding. Abdulaziz took mine from me and dolloped into it a goodly portion of something pink and slobbery, which he then formally presented to me. It was bland-tasting, not unpleasant, a bit chewy. I guessed it was some kind of pasta, as it seemed to be in ribbons, and I guessed the sauce contained a small amount of tomato, giving it its colour. After the meal, when Humphrey and I were on our own, he said, 'I'm glad he didn't give me such a pile of tripe.' Tripe? Yes, that was what it was: Humphrey, better organised and with better eyesight, had seen the menu. In one way, I was glad I didn't know. On the other hand, had I known I would have paid more attention to the experience.

There were spicy stews of lamb and baby camel. I took particular interest in the latter, as one doesn't come across it every day, and I remembered references to camel stew in T. E. Lawrence's *The Seven Pillars of Wisdom* which I had read at school. This version was very pleasant, with a flavour like a blend of lamb and rabbit. Other dishes included rice, salads, yoghurt and hot sauce. It was a memorable meal, but I wished at the time that I could have eaten it sitting at a table, in cooler air, and not in a totally stressed-out state of mind. Even in my discomfort, I worked hard to do justice to the spread and to lessen the amount of wicked waste, and regretted that courtesy required me to stop eating shortly after the others had clearly decided that the meal was at an end. I sat, if that is the word for my posture, helpless while distressingly large quantities of uneaten goodies were taken away.

The others had coffee, which I cannot touch. As we were leaving, just as we went through into the cool and comfortable interior part of the restaurant, Abdulaziz guided us to a hand washing facility. Clearly familiar with the routine, he then produced a metal jug with a rose-ended spout, from which he sprinkled over our hands a fragrance of rose-petal and lemon. The car was like an oven: Abdulaziz opened the doors for a few minutes before we got in. We discussed arrangements for future contact, and he dropped us off at the Marriott.

There, tedium happened. We had already checked out. We were booked onto a night flight, and there were hours to kill before it would be appropriate to set off for the drome. There was no alternative to hanging around in the lobby lounge. The comforts were limited: the backs of the chairs and sofas were too low for sleeping, which was probably a wise design. For limited periods of time I entered an un-refreshing, half-dozing state. I had two pots of tea. I took headache tablets and visited the toilet several times. I held some work papers in my hands and looked at them for short periods, to no great effect. The time dragged unbearably. This was my first experience of the zonked sensation that afflicts me when coming off duty after a high-stakes international assignment. Humphrey seemed content to absorb himself in something on his laptop. He was a very experienced traveller, so probably felt less physically shredded than me.

Far too early, and for want of anything better to do, we decided to take the taxi to the airport. As well as the change of scene, I imagined some comfortable facilities. When we arrived at the terminal, it was busy and confusing. We had to show our tickets and passports to get into the building, where the foyer area was a mass of people with luggage trolleys stacked high. Eventually we worked out that the check-in desks were in this foyer, and we could not go anywhere until we had checked in. Moreover, an hour and a half would elapse before the check-in for our flight would open. I was now wide awake, this scrum and confusion having removed traces of sleepiness. There was nowhere to sit down: no unclaimed space of any kind. Standing facing a pillar, I made a couple of square feet for myself, and got out the bundle of work papers I had to review and make comments on. The need to shut out the world around and create some private space gave me resources of concentration that I had not found earlier.

When we did make it through into the main body of the terminal, the seating areas were spacious. The toilets were not in a particularly nice state: Humphrey was not prepared to use them; my needs required me to be less particular. I got back to Heathrow and from there to my suburban home at about the time that people were leaving to set off for work. A neighbour commented on my arriving at this time. 'Yes,' I was happy to have the opportunity to say, 'I've just got back from Saudi Arabia'.

Chapter Four

The opportunity to go to Singapore came in September
of that same year, 2007. I only just made the flight,
having been optimistic in my timings and having suffered long delays on the Piccadilly Line. I had to move
briskly through the terminal: no time for refreshments
or to buy anything. In fact, because the gate was at
some distance, I was running the last stretch, listening
to 'final call' announcements. I would have preferred a
chance to enjoy the moment, but reflections had to wait
until I was seated. Since I was a young man, Singapore
had been high on my list of exotic places with positive,
fascinating connotations, although I had not believed
that I would get around to visiting any of them. The
events of the summer had changed my view: opportunities to travel took forms I had not known existed.

This was the case with my visit to Singapore. Over
many years a working relationship had been maintained between someone in my organisation, and a large
international school in Singapore which acted as a
training hub for a group of similar schools throughout

South East Asia. The amount of actual activity waxed and waned under different Chief Executives. Schools of this type tend to be structured with a separate head-teacher for each phase of education: early years, junior, secondary, on the same campus, so the overall leader is styled either 'Chief Executive' or 'Principal'. The current Chief Executive, Ivan, had been appointed within the last two or three years. He had done some big jobs in the UK, in a brash sort of way, and was full of big ideas. He wanted to develop a more significant partnership. He liaised with my organisation's top management, which was how he operated. I was asked to attend a couple of these meetings. It was agreed that both organisations would put some resources into exploring partnership possibilities, and to that end my organisation let me go to Singapore.

The colleague who had originated these links was a very experienced, talented and outgoing woman called Pat. A lot of her work was international, and she had built up a network of contacts willing to offer her and her associates assignments in warm and pleasant places. Her working links with the client organisation in Singapore were with Marilyn, the senior manager responsible for professional development. Marilyn made the practical arrangements for my visit. She met me at the airport, towards the end of Saturday after-noon. She escorted me with her driver to the hotel, and on the way gave me a thoroughly prepared folder including a programme of meetings. Marilyn was very pleasant and I enjoyed working with her. Later, I learnt through Pat that Marilyn had told her Ivan had shown no awareness that this kind of red carpet hospitality would be both appreciated and appropriate.

In the fading light I saw cerise splashes of bougainvillaea climbing up buildings and other structures by the side of the road from the airport. This plant gets mentioned a lot in stories set in the tropics, as part of the scene-setting, like rotating fans and the noise of cicadas. For that reason it had symbolic significance for me, and I became slightly fixated on noticing it, and looking closely at its coloured bracts. Before going to Singapore, when I read the word, I pronounced it in my head phonetically, giving each syllable equal emphasis. Marilyn told me a couple of days later to pronounce it 'buh-*gan*-villa', with the emphasis on the 'gan'. Marilyn usually booked visitors into the Traders Hotel but for some reason that option was not available, so I was to stay at a recently opened, quite small hotel that she had not used before. It was now dark, and the driver had trouble finding the hotel. He went round the same block a couple of times, then stopped and phoned for directions. Eventually I was deposited in the right place, and told to take a taxi later to the Indo-Chine Restaurant beside the harbour, for dinner.

In the course of registering my arrival at the hotel, a misunderstanding occurred. Having sorted the room, I asked when breakfast would be served, and where I would go to find it. 'No breakfast!' the man said very definitely. I sought clarification. 'This is room only!' 'Well, I'm perfectly happy to pay for breakfast or have it charged to my room account', I suggested reasonably. 'NO Breakfast!' the man shouted again, making a horizontal chopping motion with his hand at about the height of my neck. Rather foolishly, I believed him, and felt seriously incommoded because food is important to me, especially at the start of the day. After dumping things in my room I went out in search of provisions. I was already clear, from reading, word-of-mouth, and my experiences since landing, that Singapore was a fully developed, modern Western country, which was not only safe, but had virtually no crime of any kind; it was spotlessly clean and everyone spoke English. So I ambled to a general store further along the block, and bought an odd and not particularly satisfactory selection of snacks and a drink, then settled into my room until it was time to leave for dinner.

When I arrived at the restaurant, Marilyn spotted me and waved me towards an outside table, where another diner was already seated. He was one of the previous Chief Executives of the school, now retired, and visiting because he was organising a regional sporting event. From the table I had a good view of the harbour, and the air was pleasantly warm. The starters included a variation on Peking duck with pancakes: served with mint leaves and lettuce. Marilyn enjoyed demonstrating: 'Put on a lettuce leaf and some mint, now the meat, now the sauce, now wrap it ... mm!' All of the food was excellent. In a spiced dish of large prawns, even in the dark I noticed the taste and crunch of fresh ginger. The conversation slipped down just as easily. At the end of this very pleasant evening, Marilyn passed me a postcard. The picture was of a trishaw driver resting in the passenger seat with his feet up. On the reverse, in neat ink italics she had written, 'Your taxi driver is Francis. He drives a white Mercedes ... He will pick you up from the hotel at 8.00 am on Monday.' She included the car registration number, and his and her phone numbers: of limited use because my mobile phone could not make calls in Singapore.

The hotel room was adequate rather than luxurious. The small bathroom had a bath, which at that time I appreciated in preference to a shower, smelt slightly of drains, and indeed the facilities included a full-sized drain in the floor next to the bath. I was on the first floor, facing the street. One of the buildings opposite was a Chinese restaurant, whose customers appeared to be nocturnal. At whatever time of night or early morning I peeped out of the window, there would be a scattering of people at its tables.

In the morning, I went down to see whether it was really true that there was no breakfast, and was pleased to be guided by smell and sounds to a perfectly normal hotel restaurant, offering three kinds of breakfast: American, Chinese or Indian. I chose American, which was correct, because I noticed from other tables nearby that the other options were at the serious authentic ethnic extremes of those cuisines, not Westernised versions. While enjoying the egg and pancake, I looked at the Chinese waitresses briskly going about their business. I liked the way they walked. They were just concentrating on their work, not putting on any kind of show. One near to me in particular had the very slightly bow-legged, waddling gait that I thought of as distinctly and attractively oriental.

It was Sunday and I had nothing I needed to do, so could amuse myself sightseeing. I started to wander around near to the hotel, getting my bearings and finalising my plans, when I needed to hurry back inside to shelter from a sudden rain-shower. Text-book knowledge of tropical climates had not really prepared me: the amazing drenching force took me aback as tons of water fell out of the sky, drops bouncing high from surfaces which became lakes. I waited in the hotel vestibule among the orchids. There seemed to be no shortage of luxuriantly flowering orchids in Singapore: they must grow there like dandelions.

When the rain lessened to a mild drizzle, I set off to find the metro station, having decided I needed to learn how to use that excellent system. My first stopping off point was the Chinese market, housed in an enormous, busily congested marquee. Once inside, I soon felt out of place, and decided to put my camera away. This was a working place of commerce. Singaporeans are too friendly ever to look resentful, but they do have a good measure of pride, and what I noticed from people's faces was that they were affronted to be treated as a tourist curiosity. So I walked around briskly, trying to give the impression that I was looking for the stall from which I intended to buy something. The options were not very practical, and I couldn't help lingering by a stall dedicated to selling one kind of fish: I think they were large red snappers. Battered enamel dishes were set out on an equally battered table, each dish with a suitable portion. One row of dishes each offered the tail cut. Nearby, standing directly on the table like soldiers on parade was a row of heads, each propped up to show the fleshy, severed end. Other stalls sold cut flowers in great profusion, vegetables, groceries and many more: in fact Singapore's equivalent of Durham Indoor Market.

Next I went to the Old Post Office beside the harbour. The fact that it now housed the five-star Fullerton Hotel indicates the grandeur of the original establishment.

I went inside because another torrential shower was starting. In the foyer was a pool of koi, on a grand scale: something I never tire of watching. As the rain lessened, I crossed Cavenagh Bridge, passed in daylight the Indo-Chine Restaurant, previously seen in the dark, and took the boat trip with which this book opened.

Then it was time to make a decision about lunch. I walked along the row of restaurants on the other side of the harbour. Most specialised in seafood, and had their seating area outside under canopies. Their menus helpfully had pictures, showing the meals, but this was also the cause of my reservations. As I lingered, a woman would stick her arm into a tank, select a crab, and lift it out to show me, while smiling invitingly. The crab would look just as affrontedly at me as the shoppers in the market, while wriggling its legs and snapping its claws. My problem was that the pictures of the meals showed an identical crab sitting on a plate, amongst various different trimmings, this time affronted at having been splattered with great dollops of sauce. I assumed it would have encountered some boiling water on its way to the plate, but how was I supposed to get at its edible parts? The sauce being on the outside of the shell seemed to compound the problem. Perhaps Western diners were helped in some way but I did not want to take the risk, and in any case, I wanted to experience Raffles.

Raffles Hotel is quite a rambling complex. It was by now hot and sunny, and I found a suitable eating area in a courtyard: a bar serving light meals informally. I ordered Nasi Goreng and a Singapore Sling, and savoured, relished, wallowed in the sensation of being able to place that order in that location. I used to frequent the Rasa Sayang Singaporean restaurant in London, when it was more upmarket than the chain it has since become. I would have Satay, Nasi Goreng, and Tiger beer, enjoying the ambience whilst assuming it was the nearest I would ever get to Singapore. So it was fulfilling to be sitting there in Raffles. The food was of good quality but not of itself remarkable. The cocktail was pleasant: I go through cocktail-quaffing phases, but it would not bother me if I never tasted it again.

The courtyard provided a gracious setting. The building was in neo-classical style, and amply proportioned. The courtyard was surrounded by heavy arches, pillars, stone balustrades, with rows of windows above topped by pink pantiles, like the reconstructed models of Roman villas one sees next to patches of mosaic. Tropical vegetation was abundant. On peachy-pink paving stones, fancy white iron tables and chairs were set out, with plump crimson cushions on the chairs. Large butterflies flitted about, and I was keen to get a look at them, but self-consciousness kept me from actually running after them.

After lunch, I wandered around the hotel's extensive grounds, which was like visiting the central hothouse at Kew Gardens but without the glass roof. Palm trees bore clusters of great fruits that looked similar to melons. Bushes, flowering shrubs and beautiful lawns completed the scene. I ambled along the Raffles Hotel Arcade, and briefly browsed a clothes shop selling fine and stylish goods at prices beyond my means. In a gift shop, I bought a couple of bathrobes embroidered with the Raffles logo, to take home, and for myself a Raffles tie on which the logo was pleasingly discreet. After that I walked through pleasant open spaces to St Andrew's Cathedral. This nineteenth century structure in early Gothic style is reputed to be surfaced with plaster made from a mixture of eggshell, egg whites, sugar, lime and coconut husks, giving a fresh nuance to the expression 'sugar-candy town'.

On Monday morning, after another American breakfast, I met Francis in the foyer. He was tall, and had the typical Singaporean qualities of being distinguished, self-assured, and well-educated. He drove me in a south-westerly direction, along busy main roads edged with lush greenery, to the school campus. After meetings and greetings, I was given a guided tour. The most notable features of the campus were extreme spaciousness, small classes, high grade facilities, good behaviour and orderliness. There was plenty of bougainvillaea for me to look at in the grounds. I had a series of meetings with different groups of personnel. During the afternoon I received a message conveying an invitation from Ivan to dine with him that evening in the Tiffin Room at Raffles.

I took the metro and arrived in good time, entering through the grand front door under its ornamental cast iron portico. The galleried foyer was a sea of marble floor, white plaster walls, dark woodwork, easy chairs and chandeliers. Ivan greeted me and we went through into the Tiffin Room, which served an Indian buffet. It had every dish imaginable, offering the ideal spread for a many-coursed evening of manly gorging. Ivan was polite and sociable, discussing his previous career phases and current intentions pleasantly enough, but I had the feeling that he was performing a duty he had been told was necessary. I sensed that he would have perceived my status to be somewhat lowly to merit his undivided attention. He tucked into the food enthusiastically, which in itself made him reasonably good company. At the end, he said, 'My driver is coming for me. You can find yourself a taxi, can't you?' He was off, and, it being a fine evening, I walked to the station and took the metro.

Tuesday morning was set to be the important closing phase of my fieldwork. I needed to check out of my room and leave my case in left luggage. Returning to my room after breakfast, the key card would not work, despite many attempts. A member of staff came and couldn't do any better, saying something about needing to get an engineer. On the other side of the door were my working papers for the day and other things I needed. A hotel manager regretted the problem and offered me *free* use of another room in the meantime, which I explained would not solve the problem at all. Someone was going to come back in a minute, so I stayed by the door. I knew that Francis would be in reception and that I was keeping him waiting. Staying on the first floor within sight of my door, I leant over the bannisters and called to him, 'Francis!' He gazed around, looking seriously affronted at being called to in that way. I explained the position briefly. The hotel needed to get an engineer to come from some other place. Francis told the manager authoritatively, 'I think you need to get an engineer here pretty quickly!' I was agitated: having come from London to have some significant meetings, here I was stranded only a few miles away missing the appointment. I used the hotel phone to contact Marilyn, who made adjustments to the schedule. Eventually the door was opened, and my important possessions restored to me, and the morning's programme proceeded adequately.

The formalities were concluded and I took temporary farewell of Marilyn, who planned to pay a reciprocal visit to London. She was not completely at ease. Ivan managed with a firm hand, and, in common with many international schools, kept everyone on short contracts: she was not sure about her future.

From the school campus I took a taxi to the National Institute of Education, which is towards the west of Singapore Island, where I was to pay a courtesy call. During the ride I saw tracts of green landscape: I hesitate to call it 'countryside' in such a compact city state. The campus of the Institute was of modern rectangular buildings that I found stark and characterless. The visit had no purpose beyond saying 'hello' on behalf of my organisation. The person with whom I had arranged it was not there. I met a couple of people who were friendly and welcoming. We exchanged professional pleasantries for a while, but there seemed no point in prolonging the visit unnecessarily. I was imposing myself on them; they were probably busy.

There were many hours to fill before my night flight. I had chosen the Jurong Bird Park as a suitable attraction, partly because of its location near to the Institute. My head ached and I felt mentally and physically exhausted, so from the options available it also had the benefit of offering an environment where I could forget myself and relax. So I went there now, using the ever-reliable taxi service.

The Bird Park, a zoo in normal parlance, was extensive and very well presented. Of course all of the environments were artificially created, as they are in any zoo, but the effect was convincing. I rode on an elevated railway circuit ('Panorail') which provided a good overview. Then I ambled around the paths, enjoying luxuriant vegetation, fine waterfalls with pelicans standing on top, and large ponds with flamingos, sometimes viewed through the trailing fronds of creepers. There were birds from every continent including Europe. Macaws flew around freely. Large insects attracted to the environment included some of dragonfly kind. One of the walk-in free flight aviaries was the largest in the world, in which the raised walkways included a wobbly suspension bridge. On one of the slatted wooded walkways I came across what I took at first to be models of enormous lizards – dragons – with skins of unrealistically brightly coloured plastic. After I had been looking at their stock-still forms for quite a while, at close range, they moved, putting on affronted expressions. A big flock of Scarlet Ibises were approximately pillar-box red, matching a traditional red British telephone box nearby.

An eating place operated in a semi-open shed. For want of anything better to do I had a meal there, and a welcome cup of tea. The food was Western, of the meat, chips and peas variety. When I felt I could spin out the visit no longer, I took a taxi back to the hotel. Having checked out, the options were limited. In bigger hotels, you can sit around for long periods without attracting attention. Here, the only place to sit was in the combined restaurant and bar area. It would have suited me for the service to have been really slow, but it was brisk.

I had a drink, then picked something from the menu that looked light, involving soft-shelled crab, but it turned out to be greasy and filling for my taste at that moment. I drank tea as slowly as possible, but eventually had to make a move, and, far too early, took a taxi to the airport. Visiting Singapore strengthened its positive connotations. It was difficult to fault the place: it was well-run in all respects, and the achievement of developing a few square miles of silt into such a city was pretty impressive.

I presented my report; liaison continued, and Marilyn came to London in January 2008. She worked with some of my colleagues to prepare an offering of services for schools in South-East Asia. The idea was that she and I would present this at the annual meeting of the regional group of schools, which that year was to be held in Bangkok in March. Marilyn kindly arranged a school visit for me to make my trip more worthwhile.

As the time for my trip to Bangkok drew near, Ivan became irascible. He was in London recruiting staff. We met. He had assumed our discussions would be leading to an exclusive commercial relationship within the region. He had heard something implying it would not. He wanted me to agree, on the spot, that my organisation would offer his an exclusive agency for work with any of the schools in the regional group. I refused. It was impractical: my organisation had a lot of long-standing bilateral relationships, and no desire to tie its hands.

'You can't manage a partnership by making it up as you go along!', he stormed. Ivan was one of those people with the irritating habit, when they are talking at you, of feeling a need to insert your name into every sentence. On every occasion, Ivan had to pause a second, fumbling in his mind to remember my name, and then enunciating it as if it were a swearword. Over the next few days he made a nuisance of himself on my mobile phone. He wanted to talk to top management. Like others of his kind, he believed that if he spoke to someone senior enough he would get the answer he wanted. For whatever reason, he could not get through to any of them, and wanted me to make that happen. It reminded me of my days as a junior local government officer: how often, when explaining to a caller that they were not entitled to what they wanted, the reply would be total disbelief followed by 'Put me through to the Director!'

Ivan gave me more insights into his management style: 'You are coming to Bangkok as an *Invited Guest*. I need to be sure that you are going to behave properly as a *Guest* otherwise I will cancel the invitation!' 'It is *Really Important* that I get clarification from the top of your organisation *Today!*' I could not find any member of the Directorate available to speak with him. I managed a brief encounter with the person at the very top of our organisation. These always felt like encounters with a Roman Emperor, albeit of the more benign variety. This one lasted fifteen seconds. He got the gist of the matter, then, 'Why don't you tell him to fuck off?' he advised, already on his way to something important. Thus supported, I made my way to Heathrow with my mobile switched off, to prevent any last-minute dramas.

My flight with British Airways left during the evening of Tuesday 11 March, and with eleven hours of flying time, and the time difference, arrived in Bangkok mid-afternoon the following day. I was booked into the Westin Grande Sukhumvit, a hotel offering a very high standard of everything. The room was large, and the minibar surprisingly well stocked, with two different kinds of Durex condoms and half-bottles of Johnny Walker, Hennessy, Smirnoff, gin, wines, everything. From my window on a floor about half way up its tall tower, I surveyed the scene. A colleague who had travelled extensively and cheaply in Thailand had advised me, 'Bangkok will seem more like India than like Singapore'. That was a good summary. Looking eastwards, my first impression was of a forest of tower blocks, many within skyscraper category. Nearby, to the south-east, I saw the long rooves of one of the stations of what I soon learnt was an excellent system of Metro subways, and Skytrains, the latter being elevated a good way above street level. All of the spaces and cracks between these modern urban features were filled in with a down-at-heel third world clutter of shabby buildings with corrugated rooves, and street enterprises.

I had dinner in the hotel's restaurant. The member of staff who took charge of me guided me to a table and to the a la carte menu. She did not explain the various buffet options and I was too shy to ask until I had settled in. I picked a dish. To say it was chilli hot would be an understatement: it was nearly hot enough to smelt the knife and fork.

I was awake early on Thursday morning and went out exploring, in my shirtsleeves, which was daringly casual for me. I headed south-east along Thanon Sukhumvit, looked at the Skytrain station and then walked on the pavement beside this major road. The first things I noticed were the weight of traffic, and the thickness of fumes, which stung my eyes and seared my throat. The air quality, bad throughout the city, was worse at this point because the road was partially covered by the Skytrain above. At traffic lights, dozens of light motor-bikes clustered like swarms of wasps. The side streets were cobwebbed with untidy telegraph poles and wires, and lined with a wide variety of enterprises. The larger buildings included hotels and bars. I spotted a pub with a traditional English sign, 'The Bull's Head, Free House', in Old English characters with a suitable picture. This was next to a 'Home Bakery' called 'Custard'. I passed a book shop. About one in every four shops advertised Thai massage and sauna. In front of these buildings were street enterprises, many operating from parked goods rickshaws, including greengrocers and street-food vendors. Some people wax lyrical about Thai street-food, but what I saw was mainly deep-fried dough balls scented with vanilla, cooked in smelly old oil on stalls parked in the thick of traffic fumes, where the staff worked all day long with no sign of any washing facilities.

I passed a sort of wayside shrine, in an open-air triangle of ground set back from the pavement behind metal railings. On a high altar and a lower side table were ornately crafted religious artefacts, decked with flowers and garlands of flower heads, and pleasantly wafted with the fragrance of dozens of burning incense sticks. I came to the Bencha Siri Park, a sort of mini-St James's, with expanses of water features and waterfowl, surrounded by blossomy plants. The blooms were mainly cerise or yellow, with some red and white. The park included a central open shelter, and some wooden buildings in traditional Thai style. The air was fresher here. Some other early risers took their exercise, disturbing an enormous flock of town pigeons.

Back at the hotel I loitered to connect with transport to the school I was visiting. After being accosted with various taxi offers, I found the right driver and set off in one of the school's fleet of minibuses. It was luxuriously fitted out, in a strikingly smart and elaborate combination of blue and buff upholstery. The scenery was not attractive. Much of the drive was on major roads, raised flyover-style, looking out over expanses of non-descript residential development.

At the school gate, an attendant was unwilling to let me in unless I surrendered my passport, which she intended to leave on a rack, which already held a couple, in the open air beside the street, which seemed not well guarded. I refused. She insisted. I pompously explained my business and asked her to check my bona fides with her head office. After some phone calls, she reluctantly accepted a business card with my passport photo attached to it as a poor substitute.

Once admitted, I was hosted graciously and shown around wonderful facilities, with impeccable education taking place in them. A conversation with one of the teachers stuck in my mind. The doors of his classroom stood open to lush tropical gardens. Inside its spacious and perfect facilities, a class of eight diligent, clever pupils studied earnestly. The teacher said to me, 'I used to teach in a comprehensive school in Birmingham. I don't know why I made the change, really...', and he actually managed to keep a straight face. He also advised me, very usefully, that the best way to sightsee Royal Bangkok was to take the metro to a ferry terminal and approach it by river.

That evening I picked the buffet option in the restaurant, choosing mainly from the Indian selection. The quality and range of food was excellent, but I have never seen such prodigious over-provision and over-staffing. There were only a handful of diners. The buffet covered several different cuisines, in addition to offering whole salmons and large lumps of meat, with staff stationed beside them ready to carve. A pizzeria and its attendant stood ready by a blazing oven to offer a customised creation. A crepe-maker stood by his equipment and ingredients, hoping for someone to relieve his boredom. A barbecue glowed emptily. Perhaps late at night a drove of clients with post-massage appetites would turn up to justify this level of excess and redundancy. Perhaps the uneaten food entered some strata of the city's economy.

Friday was taken up with the event which was my reason for being in Bangkok. Ivan was still in London; the day passed unremarkably. He had never shown me his agreement with the regional group of schools. Marilyn thought that if a document so formal existed at all, it would not offer Ivan's training hub anything approaching exclusivity. I wondered if he was playing the asphalters' trick: 'I am asphalting your neighbour's drive, so if I do yours at the same time...', then, if you fall for it, he will go to your neighbour and say, 'I am asphalting your neighbour's drive...' In the evening I strolled into and through the Robinson department store next to the hotel. I bought a couple of the small, ornately-worked pots with lids in the classic Thai style, and a set of contemporary plastic table mats which withstood some years of hard usage.

On Saturday I had a night flight preceded by an empty day that I had planned so as to provide an opportunity for tourism. A colleague had told me that the Royal Palace and National Museum complex was an environment in which it was possible to spend a day. I checked out, and put my suitcase in left luggage. Dressed for tourism in shirt and Tilley hat, I carried a light conference-style satchel in which I had packed a clean shirt to change into on my return. A sign of the hotel's quality was that when I checked out and explained what I was doing, the receptionist suggested that I use the shower in the hotel's gym when I got back from my excursion.

Following the teacher's advice I took the Metro from Sukhumvit, changing four stops later to the Skytrain at Silom, and three stops later reaching the terminus at Sapham Taksin, on the bank of the Chao Phraya River, from where ferries departed. It was not clear where to go, and I was immediately accosted by people saying, 'You want ferry?' who I knew were selling private boat trips, which was not what I wanted. Partly to escape their attentions, I stepped onto a large official-looking ferry which in fact simply crossed the river. That wasn't what I had planned but it was interesting to have a brief look around the craft stalls on the opposite bank. When

I crossed back, the ferry I wanted was just arriving, which made everything clearer.

The river was wider than the Thames: more like the Humber. The ferry stopped very briefly at calling points, marked somewhat unobtrusively. It was a good way to see the city, with stately buildings rising behind a waterfront that varied from tree-lined esplanades, to tatty apartment blocks, to shacks and sheds of wood and corrugated iron. From my chosen disembarkation point it was easy to follow the map to the sights. On the way the streets were lined with traders. Many sat on rugs on the ground, offering selections of what looked like small terracotta mouldings: perhaps antiquities. The National Museum was fascinating, in its ornate old buildings and with elephant-shaped topiary. The exhibits were interesting too. The one room which was air-conditioned was the coin collection, and I noticed that I was not the only Westerner deciding that the coins merited prolonged appreciation. In the museum I had a simple lunch of rice-with-bits, with a welcome cup of tea, and took advantage of reasonable toilets.

Moving on to the temple and palace complex, I was overwhelmed by the rich, ornate, complex decorations of gold leaf and coloured glass mosaic covering entire surfaces, themselves intricately shaped and carved. One such surface would have taken my breath away; a whole building would have been amazing, but by the time I had seen dozens of buildings, in great variety but all equally richly decorated, I had run out of superlatives.

I was interested to see, for the first time so far as I could recall, groups of East Asian tourists walking along using umbrellas to provide shade. Perhaps that helped me to decide I had reached the point where I had been under the blazing sun for longer than was sensible, and decided to start the return journey. The sun's effect on my head may have been partly responsible for my making a foolish error of judgement. I should have retraced my steps to the ferry stop from which I disembarked. Instead I thought it would be more interesting to walk southward a bit, in the direction I needed to go, and catch the ferry at one of its stops further downstream.

I couldn't find the first stop at all. It looked clear on the map. I decided to go on to the next. On this leg of the walk, a man accosted me to tell me in English that there was a temple nearby that I could visit. I thanked him and continued walking in the direction I needed to go. He shouted after me furiously, pointing with violent stabs, 'That way! That way! That way!' as if it was inconceivable that I did not want to do as he said, and I was too tired to bother to explain. I passed through the flower market, a worthwhile sight, where it is mainly the heads of flowers which are sold, in great fragrant orange piles, for garland-making. The next ferry stop was even harder to find. On this quest I went some way down a side street where fish were being dried, which did not seem a friendly environment for tourists, and I soon gave up.

Now I was concerned. Taxis seemed to have finished for the day. Soon I would miss the last ferry. Eventually I found a clearly marked ferry stop on a piece of floating jetty. A couple of other people were waiting, with about ten minutes to spare before the last ferry hove round the bend at quite a speed. It was packed: a floating bee-swarm. I was worried that it might not stop at all, and waved desperately. It slowed alongside, and in a very un-Western manner I grabbed on to one of its poles, shoving other passengers aside to make room as necessary. Toes on deck, and hanging out over the water, I rejoiced in my delivery. In this precarious fashion I reached the smoothly efficient Skytrain, and before long was looking from Sukhumvit station at the reassuring sight of the Westin Grande, with its promise of a cool and relaxing interior.

A special kind of relief and comfort comes when you have gone pretty much to your limit, and then step into an environment that you know will enable recovery. At the end of the day's sightseeing I had absolutely had more than enough. With bursting, pounding head and aching legs, and still in my sweaty shirt, I flopped into a posh easy chair in the Westin's lounge and bar area and ordered a pot of tea. The waitresses wore tight long dresses of jade green satin, with a long slit up the side, and moved gracefully, smiling very pleasantly. The first pot of tea was wonderfully restorative; the second took the process of rehydration a stage further. Then I took up the offer of a shower in the gym. Gyms are not my scene at all, but on this occasion the facility was most welcome and the shower was intoxicatingly refreshing.

I put my clean shirt on, reclaimed my luggage, got out a blazer to put on, and sat doing nothing for a while. I noticed a middle-aged Western businessman steering a young Thai woman into the lift: an interpreter, perhaps, to help him with his paperwork. At the drome an enormous model of a mythical dragon and figures stood in a mall of fashionable Western luxury goods and indulgences. These images seemed neatly to summarise Bangkok.

Chapter Five

A few weeks later my manager told me she had been tasked with organising a conference in Beijing, to take place in November of that year, 2008, and that she wanted me to help. She encouraged me to attend the conference, which would mean my proposing a conference paper and getting it accepted. I had last presented at an international conference four years previously, in Rotterdam. I welcomed this stimulus to think afresh, but not as much as the opportunity to see Beijing. I submitted my proposal in May. Meanwhile my manager had arranged an additional event immediately before the conference: a small team in which I would be included was to run a workshop for Chinese headteachers and school district officials.

As the time for the trip approached, I learnt that I was to travel out with Louise, a distinguished colleague with a global profile, and that we were to fly business class on Air France. I met Louise at Heathrow on the afternoon of Tuesday 5 November, and we chatted pleasantly. This was the only time I have ever been booked into business class (as distinct from a couple of unexpected free upgradings), and I am glad I savoured the experience. We settled in comfortably and received glasses of champagne. Louise, in her dealings with the staff, showed off her fluent, lilting, tinkling mastery of French, which even though I could not understand some of it, was very pleasant to listen to. Needless to say, the foods and wines were of good quality and elegantly presented. We watched a film and slept.

In the morning, the views from the plane window made me revert to my former identity as a geography teacher. Low-angled morning sunlight shone on bare, rugged mountains, making a pattern of ochre on their sunlit planes and deep turquoise on their shaded sides. At first the mountains seemed to be uninhabitable, as dead as the surface of another planet. Later, the rugged peaks were separated by valleys, narrow at first, then wider, with a river and probably roads snaking between olive-tinged flat surfaces, with a faint hint of rectangular patches of farming. This landscape graduated into wooded hills of willow-pattern amplitude, each covered with a concentric contour-line pattern of terracettes. At lower altitudes there were man-made terraces using every available patch for cultivation, and these transitioned into the natural terracette landform at higher altitudes.

The flight did not offer aerial views of Beijing, the airport being some distance to the north-east of the city, at Tianzhu. I saw a patchwork of large fields, transitioning raggedly into a grid pattern of industrial and commercial development, as we started to land. Waiting on the plane to disembark, I complimented Louise because she had enabled me to cross an important milestone.

An effect of her relaxing company was that for the first time I was ending a flight without an unpleasant headache. Business-class comfort may have had something to do with it as well. Having achieved that once, it became easier to do so again on future occasions.

As it turned out, there was a real advantage in my landing merely tired but otherwise in reasonably good shape. Louise had a Chinese distant cousin. I do not think that they had met before, but she had arranged for him to meet her when she landed. When that happened, he offered to take us both, then and there, straight off the flight in our dirt and with our luggage, to see the Great Wall of China. I had assumed that my duties would not allow much opportunity for tourism so I was delighted to take up this offer. Much later, I realised that the location of the airport at a point almost equidistantly between the Great Wall and Beijing made the trip a logical suggestion.

Louise's cousin was called Chen-i. He was tall, highly educated, courteous and aristocratic. His family had been influential people playing a senior part in Chiang Ki-Shek's nationalist movement. We walked to the car. It was quite cold. I had researched the weather, and had selected two outfits accordingly. In my suitcase was a black Harris Tweed suit for formal occasions, and I was wearing more casual but equally tweedy separates including a dark green jacket and a thick shooting waistcoat, with brogues and plaid tie. It was thus immediately obvious from which island this visiting Westerner came, and I was happy that it should be so: happy to be myself, warm and comfortable.

The first place Chen-i took us to, because it was on the way from the airport, was a special kind of residence for retired people, where the residential facilities were combined with the provision of traditional Chinese medicines. The standard of accommodation and services suggested it was for people of comfortable means. Chen-i had some specific connection with the place, but I did not catch the nature of this: perhaps he had bought one of the apartments for himself. It covered an extensive campus. Somewhat in the style of a large hospital, in the car park was a direction sign with multiple arms pointing to this and that: painted bright red, with the Chinese characters in yellow. This colour scheme continued through an entrance block, modern but with traditional styling including ornately decorative painting and geometric fretwork.

Chen-i showed us the pharmacy, which was furnished with cabinets of square wooden drawers. The wood was finished in shiny dark crimson, and each of the drawer fronts had a brass ring-pull, above a red label, surrounded on the other three sides by white rectangular china tiles on which blue Chinese characters were painted. Next to this was a more workaday collection of brown paper packages stacked on metal shelves. Various forms of apparatus, made of glass, metal and china, were used for processing ingredients. Chen-i spoke knowledgeably and in detail about the practice of this form of medicine. I noted with interest the emphasis he placed on assisting recovery from illnesses. Time and again he would say that a particular remedy was good for people recovering from this or that condition: a concern less emphasised in Western medicine.

There was a richly-decorated exhibition area, displaying information and amazing items of furniture, with expanses of wood carving which were both intricate and deeply carved, giving several inches of relief. Chen-i walked us along some of the residential corridors, to show how outside the door of each apartment there was a rack for the bags of medicines delivered daily from the pharmacy, according to each resident's prescription. We passed a lounge where some residents were seated around a green-covered table, playing a game which looked like a version of Scrabble. The grounds were extensive and included gardens with pergolas and water features, designed to be conducive to mental and physical well-being. There was a white-painted arch-shaped bridge like the ones on willow-pattern china, and weeping willows, and a great rectangular expanse of water.

Chen-i gave us lunch in the restaurant at this centre. As a lover of Chinese food, I had been looking forward to eating real Chinese food in China. The lunch included soup, which was a bit like tomato soup but with glutinous congealed pieces of semi-dissolved cornflour. There were some prettily presented cold items, and a limited hot buffet which included slices of beef gristle softened by long cooking. Overall I was a bit disappointed. At regular intervals throughout the meal, one of the other diners struck his table noisily with a fly-swat.

We drove towards the Great Wall, entering an area of spectacularly rugged terrain. Rocks seemed to rise nearly vertically, yet almost to the top, spindly trees clung to every crack and crag, growing at unnatural angles on twisted trunks deformed by their unstable habitat. We began to see old sections of the wall, mainly in a ruined state, and I was astonished that anyone could build or use a wall on such steeply inclined surfaces. Of course I had no means of measuring: the stairs in my house rise at 40 degrees, and using that comparison, some of the sections of wall seemed to rise at nearer 60 degrees.

The section of wall accessible to tourists had a car park, gift shops and ticket office, with a large Chinese flag fluttering above. It was approached through a white stone arch, saying 'The Great Wall' on each side-pillar, and 'Beijing 2008 Paralympic Games' on the span. Overlooking the ticket office complex was a notice high on the mountainside, made out of white letters supported by struts, perhaps inspired by the one that announces Hollywood: this one had the Olympic slogan, 'One World One Dream'. We joined droves of people, almost entirely Chinese, walking along the top of the wall, in well wrapped-up groups, taking photos of each other against the steely blue sky.

The gradients were gentler, but still included some sections of staircase. This section of wall was restored and maintained to the extent that it felt in places like a recently re-built replica. The views were spectacular, and the sight of this famous ancient monument snaking its way across the landscape had special significance, seeing for real what is commonly seen in pictures. 'I am walking on the Great Wall of China', I said to myself, as I remembered teaching children about it, using text-books. Informative notices were displayed here and there, but we did not need to look at them: Chen-I drew upon his mine of knowledge in well-judged portions.

Satiated with this experience, we drove the fair distance to Beijing. Louise and Chen-I had a lifetime's catching up to do, while I struggled to stay awake. We came to the Jingshi Hotel, run by and located on the campus of Beijing Normal University (BNU). The hotel's sub-title was 'Centre for International Academic Exchange': it claimed, with some justification, to offer international hotel standards, and was clearly something of a status symbol for the university. My room was reasonable enough. I noticed a large drain next to the bath like the one in Singapore: clearly an oriental style in plumbing. I was not yet used to travelling, and hadn't thought much about oriental styles of tea. I wished I had brought some black teabags, and passed the visit suffering with-drawal symptoms.

I also discovered there was something else I should have brought. After the night flight and a day of sightseeing, I was desperate for a hot bath. At that stage, showers were just not my thing: I needed a tub of water. The plug didn't fit properly. I persevered, keeping the tap running all the time. When I got out, I noticed with dis-tress and irritation that the bathroom was flooded, and this had wetted the carpet beyond. The drain, whence the water came, also allowed its exit, but the following day after my room had been serviced, an officious hand-written note was pinned to the shower curtain: 'When using shower, place curtain inside the bath'. As if! I felt like writing a reply, but instead bought a traveller's plug before my next trip.

Next morning, Friday, I learnt that I was not required until a meeting at 17.00, and I decided to use this free time to go on my own to Tiananmen Square. I caught a taxi outside the hotel, which in due course deposited me beside a great expanse of hard surface. It was edged with metal railings, and behind them, trees. A great line of tourist coaches were parked along one side. There were a lot more movable metal railings stored handily for crowd control, and a high density police presence. This hub for parades and protests was one of the symbolic hearts of a vast nation. Its importance was illustrated by rows of what looked like grandly ornate street lamps. On closer view these were multi-purpose fixtures: nestling among candelabra-style rosettes of glass orbs on gold snakes-nest arms were set banks of loudspeakers. Arranged like delicate sepals below were dozens of security cameras, and, for all I knew there might be other devices to help people enjoy their visit, such as searchlights and tear-gas squirters.

That was the view to the south: for all its connotations, a vast acreage of tarmac and paving stones. Had I had the time and inclination to go on an extensive hike, I could have explored a monument and the Chairman Mao Memorial Hall to the south of the square, the National Museum to its east, and the Great Hall of the People to its west. The latter two looked, from a distance, massive, boringly extensive buildings in a grim Soviet style with neo-classical columns. Behind me, to the north, these attractions were bounded by a wide road called Dongchang'an Jie, which ran dead straight east-west, all of the main roads in this district conforming to a grid pattern. On the northern side of the road, to which I headed by means of a subway, was the Forbidden City complex, entered through the Tiananmen Gate.

I explored the parts of this great ancient site which were openly accessible, deciding that I did not have enough time or interest to buy a ticket to view the interior. The forbidden was also forbidding, with expanses of high window-less walls, painted crimson, and much of the traditional ornamental Chinese palace style of building visible only above that elevation. Although impressive in its enormous scale and 15th Century antiquity, the public areas of this complex felt slightly down at heel, as if the current regime had mixed feelings about how much glory to give to ancient dynasties.

Everywhere was crowded with tourists: mainly Chinese. I wandered through a great archway, past some parked open-top tourist buggies, into an area of ancient stone walls, a water garden, and trees with brilliant yellow leaves. Back in the main courtyard, there was a single-storey block standing by itself, divided into a number of gift shops and kiosks, offering the usual range of snacks, hats and cheap fancy souvenirs. In so many other countries it is disappointing to notice the 'Made in China' labels in souvenir shops, but here it was all genuine local produce.

A platoon-sized detachment of soldiers was being drilled. They wore tailored green uniforms, with flat-topped stiff caps that looked far too big. Most were stick-thin, and from the nervousness of their movements, recently recruited. Repeatedly, they formed up, shouldered arms, and goose-stepped. My obvious Britishness attracted attention. A young woman explained to me at length about an art exhibition which I should go with her to see, because it was showing work by students which I would be able to buy, and that would be very good. On the way to the exit, I was accosted by another young woman, who was keen to start a conversation about where I was from and whether I was enjoying my visit to China. She was staying with her uncle... I was wondering about the point of the conversation and must have looked quizzical, and certainly not in any way desirable, because she said, 'No no! It's alright! It's just that my uncle says I must speak English to people.' When we parted a few minutes later, she gave me the giggly baby-wave with which many Chinese young women say goodbye.

One of the reasons I had not wanted to prolong this outing was uncertainty about how easy it would be to find my way back to the hotel. It took a while to attract the attention of a taxi driver. Then the first one I spoke to looked at the destination on the hotel card and shook his head. Eventually I got one prepared to take me. The drive was a hair-raising, swerving attack on back-streets and short-cuts as if every second mattered. Some parts of the back-streets looked similar to those in Delhi or Bangkok with their clutter of street enterprises and bicycles. The driver avoided by millimetres the vehicles, people, bicycles and objects which flashed by, and I lost track of whether we were supposed to be driving on the right or left side of the road, as he raced directly towards oncoming traffic.

Back at the hotel, and relieved to be safe inside, I ate in the hotel buffet before getting ready for a team meeting which colleagues had organised. The food on offer was similar every day, and was disappointing. I formed a view, which grew in strength for several years, that the best Chinese food in the world is found in London. Only recently have I come to realise that what I regarded as 'authentic' Chinese food in London's Chinatown is adapted to British tastes and ingredients: tastes which do, nevertheless, seem to be shared by most of London's Chinese population.

The breakfast buffet had enough starchy items to keep me going, including chewy strips of deep-fried batter a bit like Yorkshire pudding. I sorely missed black tea, and that, with the stresses of the work, contributed to a headache which hovered at different levels of intensity throughout my stay. The breakfast buffet was adjusted and added to for the rest of the day, but was broadly similar from one day to the next. Some of the Chinese men seemed to have big appetites. The meat and fish dishes were few and disappointing, such as stir-fried chicken heads: inedible lumps of meatless splintery bone, beak and crispy eyeballs. Duck feet were another proffered treat. An array of vegetables included corn cobs and squashes which had been steamed for hours to a tasteless mush. Some dumplings looked promising from the outside, but had no filling: just solid white dumpling mixture. What particularly surprised me was the lack of flavour: sauces and seasoning were virtually absent. An unpleasant exception on the matter of flavour happened when I put something on my plate which looked as if it might have been a piece of crystal-lised fruit. As I bit into it, I realised I was accidentally sampling a so-called thousand-year-old-egg, and a dis-gusting concentrated essence of bad drains burst in my mouth.

Saturday dawned brightly, and clearer than sometimes. From my window on the tenth floor I saw metallic blue sky, above thin clouds of dirty white which faded down into beige and then umber tints at the urban skyline.

The panorama was filled with tower blocks of different heights and ages, and different degrees of ugliness, separated by grid-pattern roads, the largest of which were lined with trees. Saturday and Sunday were the days of the pre-conference workshop, in which I was to share the facilitation, as very much the junior member of the team. This was my first experience of presenting a course of this length to a group in an international setting through interpreters. Louise and the other two women in the team were all seasoned veterans. They tolerated me and I appreciated the opportunity, so everyone was reasonably content, including the participants.

There were between 35 and 40 of them, an equal mix of men and women, and mostly equipped with containers filled with cold tea. A good proportion were headteachers or local school district officials, with the number made up by some people from the university. We had a single classroom of modern standards. Some of the men wanted to be lectured at and were reluctant to apply themselves to group discussion tasks. 'We've finished', they would say, not having started. 'Lecture to them', my senior colleagues advised. That notwithstanding, as the day proceeded, the walls became covered in Chinese characters on flipcharts and post-it notes, which interpreters from the university helped us to understand. One morsel of pleasant feedback was when an interpreter showed me a post-it note and said, 'Look, that is your name in Chinese: it says that you make us think'.

The lunch, served in a cold external area, was a basic picnic: a thin plastic container of warm rice with bits of vegetables on top. The campus itself was stunningly modern. Walking from the hotel to the teaching block we were using, I passed along the front of the headquarters building. This was of white stone, eight storeys high, and the front part was set out in the form of a box laid on its side. At the front of the building, which had a fair bit of depth, two wings came forward at either side, to make three sides of a rectangle, which was covered and overlapped by a massive slab of flat roof that looked as if it was holding everything together, in the manner of a house of cards. The walkways, frequented by students on foot and on bicycles, were lined with a kind of silver birch tree that had leaves of brilliant gamboge yellow.

Sunday passed in much the same way. Registration for the conference did not open until Monday evening. During Sunday, Professor M, an ever so distinguished keynote speaker from India, put around an invitation to delegates, saying he had arranged visits to rural schools on Monday and had room in his car to take up to three people. I put my name forward for this opportunity, and was surprised, when we were sitting with the interpreter on Sunday evening going through the feedback on our workshop, to hear that I had one of the offered places.

I was more surprised on Monday morning to find that I was the only delegate to have asked for one. I met Professor M and his wife in the foyer. He had a somewhat superior air. I introduced myself. 'Are you a professor?' was all he had to say. 'No', I replied, 'I am a consultant', trying to suggest that there might just be some other respectable occupations. I need not have bothered: he only heard the word 'no', and an expression passed across his face as if I had flatulated deliberately and unpleasantly. He did not withdraw the offer of a place in his car, but was clearly disappointed that anyone who is not a professor should be so presumptuous as to request one. His wife was a normal and pleasant person, willing to talk about her time as a teacher in a rough area of London. Professor M kept conversation to a minimum.

We set off, and after a while I realised we were heading towards the Great Wall, on the same stretch of road I had travelled with Louise and Chen-i. Ruined bits of wall started to appear. We came to the first school, which was a primary school serving a district in which agriculture was an important part of the economy. People came out to meet us; the Principal had been one of the participants in our workshop. We stood about in the very chilly air exchanging greetings and looking at the external displays beside the entrance to the school site.

The school was accommodated in single storey huts, most of which were arranged in long continuous lines; others were arranged so as to create sheltered playground spaces. They looked to be of post-war vintage, perhaps 1950s, and were kept clean and smart, with signs of recent refurbishment. The large displays at the entrance were of high quality and permanent, being painted on ceramic tiles. They included details about the school, a map of China, a map of the world, and some uplifting references to Chinese culture.

I was interested in the extent of the use of external walls for permanent displays of reference materials. The outsides of the hutted classrooms were coloured white with a dado of royal blue, and extensively this blue was the background for professionally painted educational resources. Some panels were covered in writing, some had portraits of famous people, some contained scenes of places in China, and some had scientific diagrams. On buildings other than classrooms, which were mostly of red brick, large panels were attached with more information and resources in the same style.

The Principal invited us into a meeting room to tell us about the school. Few primary schools in the UK would have such a facility: it was a full-sized boardroom. It had an imposing conference table, which was set with bowls of oranges and bananas, and bowls of nuts in their shells which had been conveniently cracked, although only certain varieties were cracked sufficiently for me to be able to get at them with my fingers. The room was decorated with potted plants. We were issued with thin plastic cups of green tea.

I gained only a partial understanding of the dual control of the school by professionals and party officials. The school had far too many teachers for the number of pupils. Some had light timetables, and some were deployed as kitchen hands and caretakers: they didn't seem to mind. We were shown impressive vegetable gardens, which had elaborate constructions of bamboo canes, and healthy-looking rows of crops, and a covered section like half a polytunnel with information dis-played along one wall. We saw displays of arts and crafts, including basketwork. The kitchen cat was friendly: my clothes would have smelt of British cats.

We watched a Chinese language lesson. The children were well wrapped-up: the classroom was cold, with an ill-fitting screen rather than a proper door. The desks, chairs and blackboard could have been in a classroom in any continent. The children were reading and writing Mandarin characters; they read aloud; they took turns to write on the board. I learnt that the children were expected to know several thousand characters by a young age. The style of dress both by adults and students was very informal: this is what had replaced the compulsory battledress of the Mao era. In classrooms, the children appeared not to have any kind of uniform, certainly not from the waist up. Outside, during playtime, the majority conformed to the colour scheme of the building: royal blue trousers, and an anorak-style jacket which was white at the top with blue shapes below.

The Principal and some of the staff took us to lunch in the village, where we went to an upstairs room with two round banqueting tables. I cannot remember the meal, except that I was cold and hungry and the food was welcome. Next we drove to the Kangzhuang Middle School of Yanquing, which I can be specific about because its name board had an English translation. This offered a completely different ambience. It was a brand new two-storey building on a spacious campus, spaciously laid out, lavishly finished and equipped to a high standard. The overall colour scheme was shades of battleship grey. New school buildings that are well-resourced have a certain global sameness in many aspects, but in this case there were two features I particularly noticed as belonging to the local cultural context. The pitched rooves, finished in a modern grey material in the style of bamboo poles, turned up at the corners in the classic Chinese style. The internal layout included a courtyard, and on a couple of its sides were open-air corridors running along both storeys, linking up the classrooms. This was a style I associated with the tropics: it seemed Spartan in the cold climate here.

There were very few students around: I think the school had only just started enrolling students, and most of them had finished for the day. Those I saw were dressed in the same white and blue outerwear as the children in the primary school. We were greeted by the Principal and members of his team, who once again had been participants in the workshop. We were taken into a boardroom with the same kind of conference table, and offered pleasantries, information, apples and green tea. Then there was a tour of the school's pristine, empty facilities: a computer room, a music room, and a pottery room where, in glass fronted cupboards, classical Greek and Roman busts lined up incongruously. The outside areas were laid out in a neat rectangular pattern of grass, walkways and bicycle stands.

When I got back to the hotel, it was time to get ready for the start of conference registration, due to begin at 16.00, at which I guessed my duties would include loitering about, smiling and taking an interest. Each time I entered the lift, I passed a helpful notice, with a cartoon of a policeman, and in Chinese and English: 'Tip from policeman: no massage service in hotel rooms.' In the foyer, our partners in BNU were, as hosts, doing the registration work, with a sizable force of junior faculty and postgraduate students. I said hello to a few people and collected my own delegate pack. The top management of my organisation had arrived, and numerous colleagues who were presenting papers. At 16.45 I went back upstairs to a reception which my organisation was hosting in the restaurant. This was mainly an opportunity to explain the work we did, to a few dozen Chinese delegates who came seeking that information.

Tuesday and Wednesday were the conference days. As it was a bilingual conference, the level of real communication was affected by the skills and technical knowledge of interpreters, and by the ease with which technical concepts made sense across cultures. One Chinese expert, a fluent English speaker, summed up the last point by saying, 'We have our own ways of thinking, which are different from Western ideas'. A very elderly, much-honoured Chinaman gave a long lecture, through an interpreter, which so far as I could follow it, was a fiery, passionate exposition of communism according to Karl Marx.

The two days were just a chore to get through, without enjoyment. I had a headache throughout, and some minor organisational matters to attend to, which limited possibilities for relaxation. I did not make any worthwhile links, or talk very much to anyone. Partly this was because I could see no likelihood of any projects in my field arising from this event, but also it was because at a personal level, the sparks of rapport, of mutual interest beyond politeness, never struck. The team of colleagues I had been with for the workshop, and senior colleagues who had arrived since, were all off hob-nobbing with important Chinese opposite numbers. Or they planned things which did not interest me: one wanted to find a club where there would be salsa dancing; another needed to find somewhere to have her regular Indian head massage.

My paper presentation was the non-event I was fully expecting it to be, which is why I do not choose the word 'anti-climax'. In weighing the value of conference participation I added hardly anything to the scales for the potential influence of my paper, because that was always bound to be so slight. On this occasion, in the normal way, the papers were bunched into handy-sized groups, and each presenter given a slot of time. This one ran smoothly enough: I had about 40 minutes, which with line-by-line interpretation (of dubious accuracy) meant about 20 minutes of presentation. Of course during my exposition, some delegates were planning their own presentations to follow, or thinking about ones they had given, or daydreaming. My input generated a few short, polite discussion points: I would not have expected more. I later turned it into a book chapter, which I would not otherwise have written, which added to the positive pan of the scales. One of the closing sessions of the conference was an open discussion with a panel, on which I was a panellist. I got the opportunity to make some remarks which I thought were worthwhile and were received with interest lasting several seconds.

Banquets took place. The best was one held by my organisation for partners in BNU. We sat around rectangular tables and had reasonable food, company and conversation. The most frustrating was a lunch put on by BNU at which we were the guests. It was a smallish gathering, quite classy, with some good red wine. There were large round tables, with turntables in the middle. Chopsticks were the only utensils. No serving spoons, knives, tongs, nothing. I don't like the way that chopsticks which have been in other people's mouths are used to poke about in the communal dishes, however daintily they try to do it. Some really very good dishes came round on the turntable, but were impossible to get hold of. For example, there was a large whole steamed fish which looked most appetising, and I was yearning to get a good mouthful of it. The turntable would only stay still for a maximum of fifteen seconds before someone yanked it in their direction. How can you serve yourself a portion from a whole steamed fish using only chopsticks, at arm's length, within fifteen seconds? It was like some conceptions of hell. The accessible items were the cheap, boring bits and pieces: the desirable delicacies went back to the kitchen, mangled, smashed up, poked about, but not consumed.

The most disappointing meal was on the last evening. A special coach trip was laid on to take the delegates to a famous old restaurant which specialised in Peking duck. This was the real, original Peking duck that the whole world has tried to copy. The restaurant was up-market, way beyond the means of most of the local population. It was to be a real treat. I thought of all the beautiful, tasty, crispy versions of Peking duck I had enjoyed, from Chinatown in London, to Marks and Spencer's, to Indo-Chine in Singapore, and looked forward to enjoying the pinnacle of them all: it would be an experience to remember.

The coach tour took us around the Olympic Village, and notwithstanding that it was pitch dark, I was excited to get glimpses of the Birds Nest Stadium. There had been rumours of displacement of people's homes and livelihoods which had stood in the path of its construction, and rumours that it was to be demolished after the games, which did not happen. We came to the restaurant, were greeted by traditionally-clad staff as if we were dignitaries, and ascended a grand staircase to a series of interlinked dining rooms, where rectangular tables sat about six diners apiece. I managed to position myself with colleagues with whom I could behave naturally.

I was informed by someone who sounded convincing that the ducks were reared in some not particularly humane manner in order to make them especially fat. Then, when mercifully relieved of life, their corpses were held under running water for three days to make the fat extra slobbery. With a proud flourish, one of these delights was brought to our table. Down the centre of the platter were slices of duck, cut on the slant to maximise the fat, which comprised perhaps 85% of the slice, above a thin sliver of tasteless meat. The surface of the duck was washed with a thin brown glaze tasting of not much at all. There was no crispness or strong flavour: just slobbery fat. Around these slices were arranged bits of wing, tail, legs, neck, fried lumps of liver and other internal organs, whole webbed feet, and head: its eyes and parted beak conveying a final apologetic: 'Well, it's not my fault I am so unappetising!'. We picked at this repulsive mess, pretending to enjoy its authentic qualities.

Next morning I met up with Louise in the foyer and in due course we took a taxi, which gave us daylight views of the Bird's Nest as part of the long drive to the drome. It being a daytime flight, I saw again the barren mountain ranges, whilst enjoying Air France's most welcome Business Class hospitality. After I got back, I heard that a couple I slightly knew had been out there on a holiday to see part of the Olympics. The trip represented a major investment for them: a retirement treat which they had enjoyed. Mood, company and sense of occasion affect the experience of travel. For myself, I was sure that not for all the tea in China would I spend my own money going to Beijing as a tourist.

Chapter Six

I first met Jemima at the restaurant then called Number One Aldwych, at a lunch arranged by a couple of colleagues with whom she had corresponded. She was just a shade shorter than me. We established an easy rapport. The four of us enjoyed a convivial lunch, although Jemima sent back her seared tuna because it wasn't cooked sufficiently. I had been copied into e-mails from Jemima which were long and in an unusual style: a sort of stream of consciousness, so I was prepared to meet an interesting character.

Jemima had 30 years' experience of educational work in London boroughs with which I was familiar. She must have been a few years younger than me; chivalrously, I felt the gap was wider than was probably the case. Then she became domiciled in Yemen: not, perhaps, an obvious choice for a British ex-pat wanting to settle in the Middle East. I never got to the bottom of the reason for this move. She had a Yemeni business partner (only later did it become clear that this was purely a business relationship), and between them they ran an Arabic and English language school in Sana'a. She was well integrated into the local culture: she chewed ghat and regarded the Yemeni approach to life as unremarkable. For some of her time, Jemima worked as an education consultant. She had lately been affiliated with a Japanese consultancy. An opportunity had arisen to bid for a World Bank funded project to work with the Yemeni Ministry of Education, with whom she enjoyed cordial relations, but she had been advised that her Japanese affiliation would not be favoured: she needed to be connected with a European or North American organisation.

Hence this conversation. Naively, it never occurred to me that she might have been looking for a flag of convenience, under which to sail her ship in her own fashion with minimal interference. There was never any possibility of such an arrangement, either with me as an individual, or with my organisation, which protected the reputation of its brand. The lunch meeting had taken place about a year before my return from Beijing. We had worked on an expression of interest which was submitted in January 2008, and then on the main bid proposal, which was translated into Arabic in June 2008 for formal submission shortly afterwards. As the planning and bid-writing process had proceeded, it became clear to me that my organisation should take the lead in designing the programme, with Jemima providing essential local knowledge and local organisational support. When I got back from Beijing in November 2008, the contract was pretty nearly won, and we were planning a trip to Sana'a to clinch the deal. 'You be the man in the suit from London who comes to finalise the contract', Jemima said, and again I did not pick up the implication of these words.

Jemima set up the local arrangements for the trip, with the Ministry and the Programme Administration Unit which managed all the donor projects. The assumption was that we would sign the contract during this visit, which raised an issue for my organisation because authority to sign contracts was limited to a small number of top managers. For a while, a member of the senior team called Mary reluctantly agreed to come with me. Nearer the date of the visit, she had to pull out, which was sound judgement: she would have hated the discomforts and vagueness of arrangements, and, as it transpired, her presence would have been redundant. My organisation, through a ponderous process, gave me exceptional permission to be the signatory.

On Saturday 31 January 2009 I caught an overnight flight on Yemenia (that's not a spelling mistake: it isn't 'Yemenair') from Heathrow, via Cairo, to Sana'a. I was the only non-Yemeni on the flight. Check-in had been in a poky corner of the terminal, where, at the last minute, large parties of Yemenis with piles of baggage had congregated, excited about going home. At Cairo, the plane waited on the ground for a time while some passengers disembarked and others joined. In the morning sunlight, through a yellow ochre haze of dust, I could see the parts of the town nearest to the drome, and I took a few snaps, adjusting the lens to bring the distance nearer.

This reminded me of an incident when I was a teenager, on a package tour with my mother and brother, enduring the queasy discomfort of overnight coach travel. Going along an autobahn in the middle of the night, with rain pounding the window and further obscuring vision, the courier announced, 'the lights you can see in

the distance on the left are Stuttgart'. 'There!', said my
mother, with triumphant pride, 'now you can say you
have seen Stuttgart!' Well, here I was, now 'seeing'
Cairo. I can't resist another one of those. I was with my
wife and in-laws at a gathering that included a devout
couple who had recently returned from a tour of the
holy land, and were much uplifted by the experience.
The subject of visiting the holy land came up in the conversation, to which my father-in-law, who had served
in the Royal Navy during the Second World War,
replied, with no intended humour, 'I've been to the holy
land. We anchored off Haifa.' Whereupon the devout
man exploded indignantly with his view of what consti-
tuted a visit to the holy land. So, on second thoughts,
no, I have not seen Cairo.

At Sana'a I had to buy an entry visa. The official quoted
a price in dollars, but I had none, and Yemeni currency
is unobtainable outside the country, so I had only
pounds sterling. The official made up a price, which
seemed high in comparison with the dollar price, but
I had no option but to pay. I eventually emerged through
the bustling, confusing, entry system, and had assumed
Jemima would come to meet me in this unfamiliar environment. Instead, I was accosted by a pleasant young
man who turned out to be one of the sons of Jemima's
business partner, whose task it was to drive me into
Sana'a to the hotel they had picked for me.

The roads were busy with cars, pick-up trucks and
small vans, and bordered by an assortment of buildings,
quite a few of which were half-finished. The ground
floors were completed, from which the steel rods for
reinforced concrete poked up into the sky awaiting the

next storey. I was told that this was one of the effects of Islamic banking, which does not make loans, so the next phase has to wait.

We came to the hotel. I had no idea where it was. Before the trip I had pressed Jemima for the address of the hotel where I would be staying, explaining that my organisation expected to have this as part of the process for issuing permission to travel. Her reply had been, 'We don't really have proper addresses in Yemen yet'. My escort checked me in, assured me that Jemima would come to the hotel at 18.00, and left. My room was up a few flights of stairs. It was a cavernous, musty, suite which at first sight impressed me. I explored. Opposite the entrance hall was a sitting room furnished in a style that I later learnt was popular for ghat-chewing venues. Very low settees formed a continuous surface around three sides of the room, each seat separated from the next by a high, wide, cushioned divider. This kind of set-up enables groups of men to spend hours slumped companionably in a mild narcotic stupor.

The other rooms in the suite were a kitchen, a grand master bedroom with dark wooden furniture, a small bedroom with a single bed, and a bathroom. I put down my modest luggage and looked more closely. The grand bed was not made up: with its cover and cushions, it was simply there for show. The small bed was functional. The kitchen was also just for show: all the draws and cupboards were empty, and the empty fridge was not connected to a power supply.

The views from the windows gave me no clue as to where I was in relation to the geography of Sana'a. Both in front and to the left stretched expanses of honey-coloured buildings, mainly between three and six storeys high, and mainly of modern construction. Almost all of these blocks incorporated a distinctly Yemeni design feature: above each rectangular window was a semi-circle – either of window or of patterning. Beyond the tightly-packed buildings, mountains rose: an almost continuous range to the left, and more individual peaks to the front. Beyond the mountains, the sky was clear deep blue.

One feature of the room seemed to sum up the hotel. On the bedroom wall was a strip of coat hooks: normal coat hooks on a block of wood, screwed into the wall in the normal way. Except that whoever fitted it did not understand that it should first be unwrapped. There it was, screwed to the wall in its polythene bag with explanatory label – 'high alloy hook' – in exactly the condition it was picked up in the hardware shop. My head ached and I wanted water. Tea would have been nice, and a meal even nicer, but water was the most pressing need. I went back to reception: they didn't have any, or decided it wasn't included in the tariff, or didn't understand me. I went back to the suite, gloomily aware that I had no means of communicating with Jemima and no local currency. I established myself in the functional small bedroom, presumably designed for a maid, and did my best to sleep.

On waking, I felt it might be appropriate to wash before meeting Jemima. The water was icy cold. Feeling resentful, I performed minimal ablutions. Later Jemima explained to me that the arrangement, common in the more primitive parts of the region, was to climb up and find a switch to switch on some hours ahead of when

Saudi Arabia. Here, the women were not segregated. Social standing affected how they conducted themselves. For example, an elderly woman feted as 'mother of the revolution', who had been significantly effective in helping the current regime to shoot their way into power, and with whom we were granted an audience, had both her face and hair uncovered, in addition to some forthright opinions. The interpreters were highly educated linguists, but young and of junior official rank. They were clad in black except for an eye-slit, and of course were committed to behaving in a demur, self-effacing manner. If those cultural conventions were intended to prevent the girls from making themselves attractive, these young women had mastered the art of turning barriers to advantages. Their abayas were of a clingy fabric and not loose enough entirely to hide the figure. They moved themselves with gracefully slinky feline skill. Through the niqab slit, big dark eyes twinkled and long lashes fluttered. They spoke fluently but softly, in a bewitching Arabian Nights accent, leaning close to the ear with a hint of fragrance. And all the time I wrote my notes and acted a deadpan interest in the work of the Ministry.

One of the most senior officials was Abdul. He wanted to convey how important he was, listing all the things he was responsible for – divisions, sections, units, functions, people, money, rules – in a shouty way, pointing finger, slapping table and glaring powerfully. Time would tell whether he was open to learning anything. In another room, clearly belonging to a grand official, several young men with a cocky manner and nothing to do were sprawled around: one sitting in the grand chair; one lolling across the table. They didn't move when the senior official came in: this was obviously how they normally carried on. In another meeting, an official was expounding, surrounded by his staff, when a very old man, bare-foot and wearing grubby street-clothes, wandered in, sat down near the speaker and gazed attentively at him. No-one took any notice, and after a while he wandered out. Later I asked about this, and Jemima explained, 'Oh, he was probably an elderly relative of someone who works here. Anyone can join any meeting.'

Back with Saalim to review progress, one of his staff, Kamil, served tea. This took a while: into each glass he spooned a mint sauce-like mixture, then sugar, then poured tea, stirred and distributed them all. It was wonderful. 'Mm, Ladhidh!' I said, remembering how my Arabic tutor had told me to respond to hospitality. Kamil, who knew Jemima, became attached to our team as liaison officer. The discussions were positive. More meetings were scheduled for the following day, and then, Saalim said, 'You must come to my house at the end of the day to conclude matters socially in accordance with our customs.'

That evening I checked into my new hotel: a definite improvement on the old one. The next morning I was collected early and we had a breakfast meeting at Jemima's base. This had high walls and steel entry barriers, within which were a courtyard garden and a recent building of several storeys. The ground floor was mainly open plan. Materials for language teaching were visible here and there, but the spaces were not laid out in an obviously educational style. Two young men went out to buy breakfast, and came back with bean porridge, omelettes and flatbread. I wondered about this need to outsource the most basic provisions. I wondered (although it was none of my business) what kind of living quarters Jemima had here. We squatted on the floor and ate breakfast out of the cardboard wrappings it came in. Jemima's manner suggested that any breakfast at all was a wonderful treat.

On the way to the Ministry we passed an enormous mosque that the President had caused to be built. An odd assortment of security forces were everywhere. Some rode in pick-up trucks mounted with machine-guns. Others staffed road-blocks and checkpoints. At the Ministry our sessions included an audience with one of the ministers, who spoke fluent English and had attended a prestigious UK university. He insisted I should sample qishr, a sort of national drink make from the husks of coffee beans, flavoured with ginger and cardamom. I cannot touch coffee: it combines being a migraine trigger with causing an overall unpleasant allergic reaction. I had to weigh this knowledge against a clear diplomatic imperative, and drank most of a cup, fervently hoping that this mixture might react differently from coffee beans.

At the end of the morning we learnt that Saalim had been called away on urgent business for the rest of the day. It was a relief to be thus excused from the compulsory initiation into ghat chewing that had been threatened. We drove past the Russian embassy, famed for wild parties, to a buffet lunch at the Holiday Inn, which had recently been noted for making diners ill.

In the afternoon we drove past the old town, a famous district of traditional Yemeni buildings, on the way back to the Programme Administration Unit, where we had to report progress and to see if the contract could be signed. It could not: after being found, shuffled about, laid out on a table, and various people assembled, the view was taken that the details we had negotiated with Saalim would need to be reflected in revised wording. I was driven back to the hotel, by now feeling distinctly unwell as a result of the combined effects of stress, strange water and food, and the qishr, to perform a final duty that I had brought on myself.

There had been some issues regarding the selection of the main Yemeni member of our team, who had to be acceptable both to the Ministry, as client, and to my organisation. To satisfy the latter point, I insisted that during my stay in Sana'a I needed to meet the person. The one we had originally selected and included in our proposal – excellent and pleasant in every respect – I had already met as he had been with our team in the planning visits to the Ministry. The problem, which surprisingly had not emerged until now, was that he was employed by the Ministry and for that reason ineligible. Jemima proposed a replacement called Hassan, who lived in Ta'iz. Reluctantly, and aware what a nuisance I was being, I could see no alternative to requiring Hassan to drive several hours on the dusty, dangerous road from Ta'iz to Sana'a, so that I could meet him briefly this afternoon to smooth the way to his getting on the payroll.

The meeting was scheduled for 16.00. I had been resting, feeling migrainous and shattered. Around 15.30, I thought it would be a good idea to leave my room and go and sit in the entrance foyer, so that

I could greet Hassan when he arrived. I sat a long time, half dozing in a comfortable chair. Eventually a man approached me from behind. 'You have been sitting here; I have been sitting there' – pointing back to reception. 'Reception say Raphael is not in his room, I have driven a long way, so I am taking the initiative!' The interview took place, the formalities were concluded, and Hassan began the long drive home.

I was collected and taken back to Jemima's place for a party which began supposedly at 19.00, although it was clearly polite to arrive later. Jemima had invited contacts from the British Council, the British and some other embassies; aid agencies and some of the movers and shakers of Sana'a society. It was dark when I arrived, and my first surprise was the number and chunky character of staffed military vehicles parked at angles outside the house. The different uniforms and insignia made it look as if the armies of several nations were standing off from each other. They were embassy escorts: this was how social calls were made in Yemen. Someone told me that it was only relatively recently that democracy had reached the stage of development where it could be agreed that heavy weapons would not be brought into meetings.

Inside, there was a buffet of grilled meat, salads and flatbreads, and various soft drinks. I didn't feel like much to eat, and picked food items that I thought less likely to add to my difficulties. I chatted with a few men from the British Council: some while ago, families had been shipped home for security reasons, and it did not sound a particularly enjoyable posting. I talked with a couple of Australian women with one of the aid agencies. I took my leave of Jemima, telling her and hoping she received it as a compliment, 'You are my nuttiest consultant'.

On Wednesday morning, one of the young men came for me at 06.15 to take me to the drome. His English was as limited as my Arabic. He asked me how I found Sana'a, and I muddled my choice of adjective and said 'new', which puzzled him, and we drifted into companionable silence. I was looking forward to the relief of being on a plane bound for the UK. I found the terminal confusing, but eventually got through security, which involved detailed investigation of my luggage, and found the Yemenia check-in desk. I presented my electronic ticket in the normal way. The man seemed to take pleasure in rejecting it. 'You have not re-confirmed your flight!' I didn't know what he was talking about, and in rising panic protested that I had here a valid ticket that I had paid money for in London. 'But you have not re-confirmed your intention to travel, and the flight is full!' I explained that I didn't know anything about needing to re-confirm, and unwisely asked when the next flight was. 'Next week!' he said with relish, 'You need to go to the ticketing office!' This was pure mischief. Innocently, I fought my way back through security, against the flow, and located the ticketing office, which was shut and deserted.

I texted Jemima for advice. She replied, 'Insist'. I made my way back through security, to the check-in desk, and insisted. A senior official got involved, who told me, 'Sit and wait there and I will see what I can do.' The time passed fretfully, creeping towards scheduled departure. At the latest possible moment, the senior official beckoned me and said, 'OK, go through', and I completed passport control formalities with just enough time to run up the steps and board. There a chaotic scrum was sorting itself out and a seat was found for me. I could not remember when I last felt so relieved. We sat awhile. 'Trouble today', explained a man near to me, who had seen precedence being given to military aircraft taking off.

As, to my joy, we got airborne, the men around me became delightful companions, warm and friendly. One of them was bouncing a fretful infant on his knee, and I changed places so that they could look out of the window. I still got good views of the Arabian coast. The men worked in the motor industry in the West Midlands and were going through to Heathrow. At Cairo the changes left the plane less crowded. I got good views of the Nile Delta, and, later in the day, of the thick snow covering England.

The schedule we had agreed meant that I would need to be back in Yemen in early March to start the main phase of the project, leaving three and a half weeks in which many arrangements had to be made and materials prepared. The budget was fixed, but everything had to be approved by the Ministry, which required some costly changes; also setting up arrangements for buying and paying for goods and services within Yemen was not straightforward.

This was set to be my longest and most taxing international consultancy trip, and I was much aware at the time of what a big step this represented from the small and well-supported steps I had taken thus far. I made various naive assumptions and choices. In my travels to date I had not taken a laptop with me, and in my inexperience I was relying now on local team members having them (including the benefit of Arabic keyboards), and did not appreciate how helpful it might have been to have had my own on this occasion.

The first phase of the work was in Aden. I departed with bulky luggage, including enough white shirts for three weeks, at 22.00 on Thursday 5 March, by a very roundabout route involving a stop in Dubai, then back northwards for a stop in Bahrain, thence to Sana'a, before the final leg to Aden. Through each of these stages I snapped away out of the plane window, taking what I knew would be bad, barely decipherable photos to record these 'once in a lifetime' glimpses of faraway places. Dubai's skyscrapers and its palm-tree-shaped coastal resort; oil tankers plying the glittering water of the Gulf; Bahrain's extensive industrial landscape (is it just a gigantic oil depot? No, I saw residential areas eventually) and the long causeway linking it to Saudi Arabia; and finally the parched brown hills of Yemen, until one of the flight staff told me, 'Stop that, it's not allowed'.

My suitcase took forever to appear: I was left waiting anxiously long after everyone else off the flight had gone, whilst answering a security official's questions about what I was doing there. I was met by a driver and taken to the 'Sheraton' Gold Mohur Hotel and Resort. That was the name in large letters along the roof, but it turned out that the hotel no longer had any right to the Sheraton label. That notwithstanding, it was of international standard and had interesting grounds and a private beach. This was to be the lodging and training venue for an intensive training experience we were providing for a group of Ministry personnel, mainly men and a few women, who were responsible for leading change. The programme would run from Sunday to Thursday, after which we would go to Ta'iz for the next piece of work. I arrived in Aden towards the end of Friday, leaving Saturday to get everything set up.

My room looked out over the bay: the Gulf of Aden, part of the Arabian Sea, part of the Indian Ocean. I thought the view was spectacular and exotic. I kept taking photographs of it at different times of day and in different lighting conditions, because it seemed to change so much. The natural features of the bay gave it scenic interest: headlands either side, a small conical hill, and various islands a short way out. The whole scene was dotted with palm trees: whether natural or planted I could not tell. There was a fine beach with a small pleasure-boat moored. There was always plenty of shipping moving through the islands to or from the port.

In the foreground of the view from my window was the external portion of the hotel site, including gardens with paths and various outside eating facilities. These and the private beach were enclosed within stout security walls either side, marking the boundaries of the site and extending into the sea. Perhaps for people staying as tourists these barricades might have taken something away from their sense of holiday fun. I felt no objection to being within such a well-appointed prison.

During my stay I wandered around the gardens and on the beach, on my own, on numerous occasions. Large numbers of crows, of similar size and behaviour to jackdaws, made these grounds their home, investigating bits of rubbish. Some of the palm trees were laden with heavy-looking fruits. The beach seemed to be made mainly of abraded thin white coral; I brought a few samples of it home with me. The bay had the effect of making the sea very calm with placid low waves, which when lit by the sun shone with a shade of blue similar to glacier ice. Sometimes the sun was glaring, and the heat intense. On one such occasion, although I was dressed for work not leisure, and when I thought no-one would see me, I slipped my shoes off and let the sea wet my feet for a few minutes, in this small way making real my contact with this exotic seashore.

On Saturday I met up with Jemima and Hasan, and an interpreter. We checked and adjusted the training room arrangements, and made up packs of materials. There was no writing paper for the participants, and the hotel did not provide it. We would need to go to the souk to buy some. The souk did not really get going until dusk – shopping is done at night in Yemen. Kamil had arrived by this time and joined the party. Hassan had brought his car with him; he was very proud of having this luxury and offered to drive us to the souk. It had character and charm, being of classic car vintage, with bodywork battered into crookedness, and bullet holes through the windscreen. As we got going it became clear that second gear was the highest one functioning; by revving furiously Hassan attained reasonable speed. The souk was a maze of narrow streets with a chaotic variety of shops, small kiosks, stalls and individual vendors. An unlikely source of stationery was found, and Jemima and Kamil went to do the bartering.

When the purchase was completed, Jemima suggested a drink in the hotel owned by the Bin Ladens: that is to say, it was owned by the Saudi family of which the terrorist Osama Bin Laden was a member. It was interesting to see the place, on the sea front, but once we had got in and found the bar we were told it was available to resident guests only. So we stopped at a juice kiosk on the beach. Unwisely I joined the others in having a freshly-squeezed fruit drink. It was a pleasant ambience, although too dark to see much. A strong breeze blew towards the sea, in reverse of the daytime pattern as the land heated and cooled more quickly. Waves could be seen and heard breaking on the beach. As well as juice kiosks, this stretch of beach had providers of the pipes called variously hubble-bubbles or hookahs: the kind that stand two feet tall and produce fragrant clouds. The vendors had glowing braziers of charcoal for them.

On Sunday the programme got off to a good start, considering how new it was for everyone and that our team had also not worked together before. Saalim's quiet authority ensured the compliance of the other participants. Predictably, Abdul threw his weight about. The battle he picked concerned his criticisms of word choices and grammatical forms in the Arabic translations of the materials. Some of his issues were undoubtedly valid, notwithstanding that we had had the translation done by a Yemeni with technical expertise, but some would have reflected a recurrent problem of certain concepts not translating easily from English to Arabic. He tried to demand that the programme should not proceed until everything was corrected to his satisfaction. Gently I explained to the group that despite their exalted positions in their day jobs, for the next week they were students, and I and my colleagues, their teachers.

We did interactive group-work tasks of a kind that were alien to the participants' respectful, hierarchical culture, and gradually saw the younger, brighter members of the group gaining confidence in speaking up in front of their elders. We organised a fieldwork day, to visit schools in groups as part of a task. Other visits were discussed, and it was clear that the senior members of the group saw it as politically imperative that in the afternoon, the whole group should visit the School for Nature. This sounded interesting: something to do with environmental education?

On the school visit day, we set off together in a couple of small coaches, from which each group would be dropped at their school. Aden appeared to be built on an interesting geological area, probably of volcanic rock, which had been eroded into a series of jagged promontories, inlets and islands. There were a lot of steep hills into the sides of which buildings were stuck in some way, and whose occupants must have had confidence in whatever form of glue had been used to do so. The Gold Mohur area is a peninsula. Any journeys from the hotel involved taking the road along the narrow neck which joined it to the mainland.

There were parts of Aden where effort had been put into creating the pavements, gardens and ornamental features that might remind one of a British seaside resort. Most of the town, however, seemed to be a higgledy-piggledy muddle of buildings of different kinds and qualities, always separated from the road by a no-man's-land of dust and rubble. Traffic was quite heavy: mainly four-wheel drive vehicles. The town was busy with people. The women were all black-clad and fully veiled; the men mostly wore a distinctly Yemeni mixture of Western and tribal dress.

I went with Abdul's group to a secondary school, which by the standards of the region was well housed and equipped. The (all male) students were dressed in Western style white shirts and black trousers; there were displays on the wall, and the school had a computer room. In the meeting with the Principal and his senior team, instead of practising the observing and data-gathering skills with which the exercise was concerned, Abdul adopted a demanding and overbearing tone, firing hostile questions. When we went into a classroom, the students stood. Abdul ordered them to sit. Then he ordered them to stand again. Then sit, then stand, and sit and stand, until his amusement was satiated.

The coaches collected the groups and went to a restaurant where lunch had been arranged. The coach I was in arrived ahead of the other. There was a group of black-clad, hijab and niqab-covered women outside the restaurant, and as we passed along the line, it became apparent from their propositionings that they were prostitutes: a cause of embarrassment to the Yemenis in our party. It seemed we would be waiting a bit before eating, so I thought a toilet visit might be a good idea, and asked a member of the restaurant staff for this in my beginner's Arabic. Surprisingly, he understood, and led me on quite a long walk, to a clean, well-hosed hole in the floor.

The meal, which turned out to be one of the better ones I experienced in Yemen, included good sea-foods spoilt by being encased in thick breadcrumb coating and fried in dirty old oil. Next was some very good roasted young lamb, served in big hunks to pick apart at the table: a messy and competitive process.

When we came out of the restaurant, the prostitutes were still there, and gathered around the minibus after we had got in. Abdul shouted and gestured angrily at them, passing a paltry banknote through the window. From the way the other men laughed I imagine he said something like 'go fuck yourselves!' I thought this was a harsh and unappreciative way to relate to feminine charms, even if you don't want to buy them. I was looking at the girl outside the window from me: at her eyes, the only part visible above the veil, which were pretty and alluring. She saw me looking, and with a gesture towards the hostile Abdul, recognising his authority, gave a beautifully expressive shrug with a merry twinkle that said, 'your loss, habibee!'

The next event on the schedule was the visit I was much anticipating to the intriguing School for Nature. I thought this might be in a rural spot outside the town, but we seemed to be heading to an industrial area. I was sitting next to Hassan and asked him, 'What is this School for Nature we are going to?' He looked at me a little oddly, and explained, 'Well, it is where the school desks and chairs are made.' So, wondering how much else I was misunderstanding through accented interpretation, I disembarked with the others and headed towards the headquarters and factory that supplied school furniture.

I was walking behind some of the men in the group, four abreast. They were having an enjoyable day, and with the innocent happiness of children in a playground, they joined hands in a line and adopted something approaching a skipping gait. The factory was a bustling clamour of machinery, materials and third-world disregard for health and safety. After a boringly long tour we went to a headquarters building for a discussion with the management: this was the meeting some senior members of the group had regarded as necessary. The point at issue seemed to be whether this production unit had to stay as part of the Ministry, or whether it could be privatised so that the people who ran it could make profit. The trip around the factory had left everyone hot and thirsty. In the meeting room were many bottles of water but no glasses, and after a while all of the bottles had been opened and used haphazardly, so the choice was between staying thirsty or drinking from a bottle that had been gobbed on by someone else.

Back at the hotel, there was the usual need to decide where and what to eat. I was mostly on my own. A further team member I had recruited in London had arrived on Sunday evening, and she and Jemima liked to go into the town in the evenings. I had recruited this team member at a late stage to satisfy the Ministry's requirements regarding the mix of experience. Thus she had me over a barrel, and charged high fees for the few days she could spare, and made little input. She left Aden before we did, but whilst there kept Jemima company.

The hotel buffet offered an acceptable basic range, but it was generally the same from each day to the next and

I wondered how long some of it had been sitting there. There were some other eating places in the hotel grounds, but we were there out of season and they looked pretty much shut up. One of these was a fish restaurant, and we went there for the only evening meal I recall us taking together. The staff assured us it was open, wiped the dust from a table, and after a while brought us a reasonably good grilled fish. Another of these outbuildings purported to be a Chinese restaurant. My stomach had become upset a couple of days into the trip, in the usual manner, but that did not keep me from having a healthy appetite. On the Wednesday evening, against my better judgement, I wandered into this outbuilding to see what was going on. Although clearly inactive, a member of staff appeared and was eager to serve me. I chose from a basic menu and after some wok-bashing the offerings arrived. The predominant flavour was Thai fish sauce, which Chinese restaurants never use, and the other ingredients were unexciting.

A couple of hours later, in my room, I was beset by vomiting and feverish shivering, and took to my bed assuming that these were symptoms of food poisoning. My arrangements made no provision for being out of action through illness, so I was keenly interested in how things might progress. After a night of violently dispelling things from my body, I faced the last day of the programme in a weak and watery condition. It went pretty well. In our timings we had assumed that participants would want an early getaway, and would have planned their flights accordingly, but Saalim insisted that the programme should continue to the normal finishing time. Participants and presenters shared the deadly experience of trying to fill in this period when there was nothing left to say.

On Friday morning I went to check-out, ready for our planned departure at 10.00. I felt far from well: still feverish, head aching and buzzing, and digestion all over the place. I went through the check-out routine. Jemima was doing the same, a few yards to my right. I was offering my credit card, but the receptionist said, 'The bill has been paid by your company'. I queried, she was sure. Foolishly, I assumed this was Jemima's doing: either her organisation was acting as banker, or she had set up pre-payment with my administrator in London.

Chapter Seven

Jemima, Kamil and I set off from Aden in a minibus with a driver. Kamil had arranged our travel papers. We had to keep to the main road between Aden and Ta'iz, and we would be checked in and out at a series of army checkpoints along the route. Once we left the town, notwithstanding my discomfort, my eyes were glued to the window and the passing desert scenery.

This started off as a fairly flat expanse of sand, with occasional small clumps of some tough kind of grass, and a few stunted bushes. The ground became more undulating, with bushes rather than grass poking through the sand at more frequent intervals. These undulating ridges progressed into sand dunes: hilly and looking very soft, spilling onto the road in small dusty avalanches. The dunes were dead and deserted under a hard blue sky, and wanted only the addition of a camel rider to match my mental image of Arabia.

Some miles farther on, the dunes gave way to a rocky landscape that became increasingly mountainous. Often the strata of these bare, wind-polished rocks were clearly visible, offering potential clues to the history of the area in their upended, twisted, faulted patterns. For one stretch, the road seemed to be following the course of a wadi which had cut an incised channel, in which there was green vegetation. On both sides were wide terraces of stony ground and thin scrub, on one of which the road ran. On the other were occasional signs of human activity. Here and there, low, roofless ruined buildings; in another place, a settlement comprising a cluster of small windowless blocks and something that looked more recognisably a building, with odd structures on its flat roof. Behind, the mountains were rising more jaggedly. We passed through a couple of more substantial settlements: Arab-style wild west towns, which is where the army checkpoints were.

As we got nearer to Ta'iz the landscape changed, becoming more settled and cultivated. I saw a field of maize and a cart-track to a farm, winding between fields of some other crops, and people bumping over the dusty ground on motorbikes. Then the views became more dramatically mountainous, with masses of dark green trees and shrubs in valleys and on sheltered surfaces. There were still plenty of patches of bare rock, sand and desert scrub. Traffic and buildings started to increase. Approaching the town the road was cut into the side of the mountain, much protected by concrete reinforcements and tiers of steel piles. This road seemed to be a major civil engineering investment, and an attempt had been made to beautify it: the central barrier between the carriageways was finished in high-grade ornamental stonework, including rectangular planters all the way along. These were mainly empty; a few were growing weeds.

The accommodation we had originally booked for the Ta'iz phase of the work had been ruled out by the Ministry because they judged its site too difficult to defend. At a late stage the venue had been switched to a hotel set at a high altitude overlooking the town. The final stretch of the journey was a spectacular drive up the side of a mountain, on a road with hairpin bends and steep gradients in the style of an alpine pass. Later someone told me that the construction of this road had been a gift from one of the wealthier Arab states. Finally we came to the hotel and got checked in. There were no other guests. The man doing reception (I think he did most things except the cooking) needed to photocopy my passport. Good hotels do that quickly and give it back to you. Irritating hotels insist that they will bring it to your room 'shortly', a practice I detest. What if they don't? What if they leave it in the wrong room, or forget about it, or drop it in the shredder, or later deny they've ever met me?

Reluctantly I parted from it and went to my room. The others knew that I was feeling slightly under the weather, that we were basically off-duty for the next 24 hours, and did not expect to see me anytime soon. 'You'll just want to crash out', Jemima said. I entered my room and found the bathroom: a matter of some urgency to me. I wished the manager would hurry up with my passport so I could relax and have privacy, but he was taking too long. I couldn't wait. Normally I did not lock hotel bathroom doors (and now never even fully shut them), but I thought it would be polite to do so in the circumstances of an expected room visit. You know already what happens next in this story.

After an explosive, much extended and sourly suffocating evacuation, I found that the door would not unlock. No amount of fiddling would make any difference. So, there I was, locked in a stinking bathroom with all my possessions out of reach, and everyone assuming (quite wrongly in any circumstances) that I wanted not to be disturbed for the next 24 hours. I felt rising panic, and only after futilely shouting and banging on walls, noticed a telephone on the wall. After a lot of trial and error stabbing at the keys, I was able to inform reception of my situation. A couple of men came: of course they thought it was some trivial fault on my part, but something had broken and it took about 20 minutes and various tools to release me, but even after that time the atmosphere in the bathroom was still a cause of embarrassment.

Relieved in every way, I explored the place that would be home for the next two weeks. That may not sound long, but, anxious as I was about all the things which could go wrong on this assignment, that period stretched ahead like a prison sentence. My room was large. The main part of the hotel had windows only on one side, being carved into the steep mountainside. The door from the corridor, which ran along the dark side, opened into a spacious seating area extending to the windows on the far side. It had a table and chairs, then further on a suite of easy chairs around a low table. Part way along this lounge, a flight of six steps rose to a split-level sleeping area, separated from the lounge by wooden bannisters. That contained a bed, more easy chairs around a coffee table, and a desk, at which I spent many boring hours. A door off the bedroom led to the bathroom. This was the Jabal Saber Hotel, which according to a guide book was originally a gift to the Yemeni Government from a UAE sheikh whose ancestors came from here.

The view from the window was spectacular: a word hard not to keep repeating in relation to Ta'iz. If I looked down, I saw the snaking course of the road by which we had arrived: the view including four hairpin bends, eight steep straight-ish sections between them, and massive concrete reinforcements holding the road and the cliff faces in place. High on one of these structures was a neatly painted motif, put there by a graffiti artist with mountaineering skills. In white paint, it showed two horses prancing on their hind legs, facing each other, with matching marks like ticks above. I was told it was the symbol of a political organisation.

If I looked down and to the left, there was the city of Ta'iz, a long way below, nestling in a valley between two mountain ranges. Up to the right was the rugged crest of the mountains, not so much higher than the altitude of this hotel. There was a building right on the top, and all the way up a scattering of traditional Yemeni buildings: of small square section but four or five storeys high, clinging to impossibly steep sites. The ground between these houses was a chaotic clutter of massive rocks and many parched-looking trees, with no visible tracks: it was a mystery how their occupants got to them. Straight ahead were mountain tops beyond mountain tops: green and brown, then warm grey, then blue, behind which the sun gently set.

Jemima and Kamil invited me to join them for a meal in the town, with someone they both knew: a young man who was getting married in a few days' time. A taxi was organised. The restaurant had tables beside the road, and served barbecued meat and flatbreads. A friendly cat rubbed expectantly against the table leg. There was some talk of politics – the young man expressed frustration at the postponement of the elections. Then the conversation turned to his forthcoming marriage.

He told us that the actual marriage ceremony took place between himself and the bride's father. Had he seen his bride? Yes, he was very fortunate in that respect: the families had enabled them to meet and they liked each other. But he emphasised that this wasn't a big issue for him. He trusted his parents to make an excellent choice for him. He deplored the practice of some of his friends, who had insisted on seeing their bride's face before agreeing to marry: that was really disrespectful to the girl, to want to look her over in that way. With typical hospitality, he invited us to attend, but it was on a working day.

On Saturday I set off at 09.00 to go with Jemima and Kamil to visit the provincial Director of Education. This was to arrange fieldwork days for the two groups of Ministry personnel we were to work with. I planned to set them things to find out and think about while visiting schools and local education offices. I was worried that senior officials would be familiar with the regional and local offices and would resent the task, but in the event that was not an issue: they didn't get out and about much. The office we went to was busy with a lot of staff and apparent activity. Hierarchical protocols were strong. We got audiences with the senior people who were helpful.

Back at the hotel, just as dusk was falling, a power cut occurred, and as it extended, it became obvious that this was a significant problem. As I noted earlier, the side of the hotel against the mountain had no windows in its lower floors, so without electric light these corridors were plunged into total blackness. Important people from the Ministry were starting to arrive for the programme which began the following morning, and weren't too impressed. The programme was, incidentally, designed on the assumption that there would be electricity for laptops and PowerPoint. The hotel manager said that he was getting on to the Grid to sort something out. Later, he explained that actually, the hotel wasn't currently connected to the Grid. It had come off some while ago following a disagreement about charges. The hotel was dependent on its own generator, which had broken down. The manager stood in reception handing out candles, with the air of offering good personal service: each candle lit with his own cigarette lighter and handed to a guest. Nothing to stand it in, and as I took mine to my room I was fully expecting that the next emergency would be a fire.

On Sunday morning, with power mercifully restored, I was involved in the last-minute rush to get everything ready for the programme. Somehow we made a reasonably dignified start. Saalim and some of the others from the Aden programme were in this first batch, which helped a sense of authority and continuity. During the first tea break, my rising sense of confidence and happiness was set back by Jemima bearing a message: the hotel in Aden was on the phone, saying that I had left without paying my bill, and I had better speak to them. I took the call, explained how I had legitimately checked out, offered my credit card, and been assured that the bill had been paid. No, after my departure, they had discovered that was a mistake. We started, and continued in several subsequent telephone conversations, exploring the options for how I could settle this debt. I was very clear that if I did not do so, I would not be leaving Yemen.

The first suggestion was that I should photocopy my credit card and fax it to them with a statement authorising payment. Even if my current hotel's equipment was up to the task, I couldn't imagine the credit card company authorising the transaction. Then we hit on the idea of me crediting the Aden hotel's bank account at a bank in Ta'iz. This sounds so simple, but the first obstacle of many was that for the next three days, during banking hours, I was committed to working with the group.

That work was tiring. I was only slowly recovering from the severe gastric upset. The hotel was at an altitude sufficient to leave me panting after climbing stairs. Bottled water was in limited supply. I yearned for gallons of tea, but the tea on offer was a red, sweetly-spiced, syrupy mixture served in tiny cups. In other circumstances this might have been a delicious treat, but I found it cloyingly inadequate. One evening I approached reception in desperation, phrase-book in hand, to try to explain my need. A few days later I learnt the magic words, but at that moment the staff chose not to understand me. The more ways I tried to say 'No sugar', the more they said. 'You want extra sugar?'

The hotel's ambience was, however, a continuing treat of breath-taking views, and, nearer to, interesting vegetation bathed in scorching sunlight. The uncultivated areas had scrubby olive-green bushes and stunted trees, and cacti including large prickly-pears, and various succulents. There were some semi-cultivated terraces, as if a helping hand had been applied to natural terracettes, and some of these seemed to be growing dark green shrubs which could well have been ghat. The areas of ornamental planting, around the hotel and some of the other larger buildings, included tall, very slim conifers – a form of cypress – and patches of a shrub covered in brilliant cerise flowers. During one break I enjoyed watching exotic butterflies visiting these.

The hotel was provided with a massive majlis, or ghat-chewing palace, big enough to be a hotel in its own right. It was a two-storey building, approached by a raised walkway joining the hotel to its upper-storey entrance. Once the delegates from the Ministry had arrived, the hotel was made secure. This distinction was somewhat pointed: the spirit of this contract was that if I and my team wanted security, we had to arrange it and pay for it ourselves. Now, heavily armed soldiers lounged around outside. The Yemenis chewed ghat after lunch and again in the early evening. By working hard at this, and bulging out their cheek with an enormous ball of the stuff, they could become significantly intoxicated. By mid-afternoon the soldiers were slumped over their Kalashnikovs, which I hoped had their safety catches on, and out on the hairpin bends people would drive their battered old vehicles in a crazy fashion.

Ghat was a consuming passion among virtually all Yemeni men, and quite a proportion of women. It was the first call on family income, and, I was told, the only crop in Yemen to be irrigated. One day after lunch I noticed our interpreter showing off some particularly good leafy sprigs he was pulling out of a paper bag, like a suburban gardener boasting about his privet.

My colleague Gordon arrived from London on Monday. I had been looking forward to his companionship. This was the first time I had worked with him on an international assignment. I liked Gordon because he was an interesting thinker, and a very kind man: someone with whom I could relax. That did not really describe my relationship with Jemima. I liked her and would have valued her friendship and company, but she kept her distance, co-operating as necessary on professional matters but with what I detected as a slight underlying resentment. By and large she didn't go much out of her way to make me feel at ease in her country. For example, I had to get my passport stamped within a certain number of days of arriving, in breach of which there would be problems when I tried to leave the country, including the certainty of paying a fine. I asked Jemima a couple of times how I should get this stamp, but she just said, 'No-one bothers to get them on time.' After raising it a few more times, Kamil kindly took my passport to a police station and got it sorted.

She did, however, organise a memorable trip to the Shannini Market, in the old town, on Monday evening. It was packed with jostling people, and I kept near to the others, and my hands over my pockets. It was dark, being night, but for much of our visit there was also a prolonged power cut, and I realised afterwards that this intense blackness, and the spirit of animation that power cuts generate, added much to the atmosphere.

We spent a while looking at crafted silverware. One of the party wanted to buy a jambiyya in a silver scabbard, during which transaction the shop served us all with mint tea. We walked along a narrow street with stalls and booths along both sides, lit with an odd assortment of lamps, candles and improvised flaming spills and torches. In the dark, the blacksmith's shop was particularly visible: the furnace casting a red glow over the faces of people forging red-hot bits of metal. Elsewhere there were other crafts, foods, clothes, and a special local kind of cheese. Gordon said he planned to come back in daylight.

Tuesday was the fieldwork day, and once again I assigned myself to the group which included Abdul. We were to learn about the work of one of the local school district offices serving part of the rural fringe of Ta'iz, in whose area the hotel was located. This started by visiting a school a short walk away from the hotel. Leaving the road, a path which was hardly a path at all led between dwellings, down rocky slopes, among bushes and outcrops of rock.

Seen at close quarters, the mountainside had been much worked on to make it more convenient for habitation. Almost everywhere, patches of traditional dry stone walling helped to retain soil in place and provide paths. The gradient was steep, so progressing downwards we passed the tops of houses, which was often where cooking was done. Close-up, the ancient stonework was offset by the use of corrugated iron, breeze blocks and gas bottles. Walking so near to people's homes felt intrusive.

The path reached the school at its lowest point, so it towered above, although its main classroom block was only two storeys. The building looked fairly modern, but constructed with traditional Yemeni styling. The classes were mixed, with boys and girls sitting separately in the same room. High on the walls, above the children's reach, were various educational displays that the teachers had made themselves. By third-world standards, the facilities were reasonable. The school had a dozen or so staff who related well to the children and each other. The world over, some schools are happy; some are prisons: this one was happy.

We went to the local district office nearby, but this had only two small rooms with no furniture. The main district official was there on his own and it was agreed that the discussion would happen more comfortably back at the hotel in the ghat palace. As the meeting assembled, a few more of the district staff appeared. It seemed that a large team of staff were on the payroll, but with no real duties, and no equipment: the district office had one computer, which one of the team kept in his home. If they tried to interfere much with the schools, they said they would be overruled because people would appeal to higher levels of government. Abdul questioned them sharply on these matters.

The next morning, Gordon was out early, and being both a seasoned traveller and more sociable than me, had been exploring the village. This was just up from the hotel, around the next hairpin bend. He mentioned a sweet shop and I walked up with him to see it. This section of road was lined on both sides with small shops made out of concrete slabs with heavy metal doors. Some were just like garages; others a bit more sophisticated. Four storey buildings rose at intervals above the shops, and small goats wandered in front of them. Gordon pointed to where he had met the woman who was the local senior ghat-dealer, collecting money from more minor dealers. At the front of the sweet shop was a large cauldron of hot melted sugar, to which colour and flavour had been added, and which a young man was stirring dramatically with a wooden paddle. On shelves were round cakes of the sugar, and various finished confections. The place smelt appetisingly sweet and spicy, but we did not buy anything.

During the working session, the matter of regime change in Iraq came up: a sensitive subject for people who would be seen, however inaccurately, as representing the British Government. I had had the chance to meet and talk in London with Ministers from the new regimes of Iraq and Iraqi Kurdistan and had heard about their daily context of carnage. Abdul took the opportunity to declare his admiration for Saddam Hussein, and his profound regret that he had been ousted from power. The work included much on leadership development, raising again the problems of translation. At one point, one of the older members of the group looked at me very darkly, and said, 'We get our leadership from Mr President, so what are you implying?'

At the end of Wednesday, the first batch of delegates departed, and the next programme would start on Sunday, leaving three days of discretionary time. I was mindful of my unpaid account at the hotel in Aden. Jemima had said it would be an easy matter for me to go to a certain bank in the town and credit the hotel's account from my credit card. Reluctantly, she agreed to come with me, and I was glad in a way that she was able to witness the bank official explaining that they did not do that kind of transaction: the account could only be credited in cash, which I did not have in anything like the quantity required. Jemima did not suggest any solution.

Later, Gordon, with typically caring concern, said that he was anxious we should resolve the matter. He floated the idea that we might even need to make the journey back to Aden, although organising that would be complex because of the need for official permission to travel, and expensive. He kindly offered to draw cash on his own cards, which we could settle up later. The hotel manager needed to do some things in town and offered to drive us down and back. The same bank as before had a cash dispenser outside. After becoming familiar with how it worked, Gordon produced some US dollars; I used my own cards to produce some more: between us the transaction limits on various cards enabled the required sum.

This strategy was not without risks, starting with all the things which might happen as a result of sticking one's cards into a machine in a foreign country. Also, at that period, I was not financially comfortable, and having to use my personal cards for substantial business trans-actions, which might not be repaid for many weeks, made me worry about my credit limit and overdraft. Finally, Yemeni institutions were very fussy about which particular dated issues of US dollars they were prepared to accept, and it was not at all improbable that the bank might refuse to accept the notes which had just come out of its own cash dispenser. Fortunately that did not happen, and I came out of the bank with a great weight removed from my shoulders.

Some of the street scenes in Ta'iz seemed, to my inexperienced eye, to have much in common with some of the townscapes in India and Thailand, especially in the absence of pavements, the small road-side shops and stalls, and the variety of vehicles. Certainly the driving exhibited what I was coming to think of as a distinctive third-world skill in avoiding collisions in chaotic conditions, which included lax ideas about rights of way, and an absence of lane discipline. The one exception was the respect paid to speed humps. To my surprise, all vehicles slowed virtually to a stop to cross these obstructions, which presumably were capable of inflicting more damage than the ones in the UK.

Motorcycles were everywhere, and on one of the trips into town, I saw just in front of us one with a rider who had a calf laid across his lap: not a tiny new-born – this was a substantial burden. At first I assumed it must be dead, to be lolling so placidly, but as we passed I saw it moving its head about, taking an interest. Another time, our progress was held up by a street funeral party, of the kind I had seen previously only on television coverage of violent events. An animated crowd bore a crude coffin aloft on its jolting unstable journey, and took it in turns to climb on each other's shoulders to dance around shrieking and waving.

On the drive back from the bank, the manager stopped to pick up a large bag of flatbreads from a shop. This explained why the ones served at the hotel were often dry and stale: they bought them in, and worked through the stock. The food was unexciting generally. On working days, a buffet lunch was provided in the conference suite. For all other occasions, there was a limited menu which never changed. The main eating area was an open roof-top terrace with views over the city. After exploring the limited options, I settled on egg and chips as the safest breakfast option. The chips were clearly out of a freezer pack and the eggs were unexceptionable. Often this was presented with no cutlery. Usually Gordon and I would take breakfast together. I had learnt from him to ask for Lipton's tea. They had a supply, and knew to serve it without sugar or added flavours.

For lunch and dinner, the several options included liver, or chicken, or lamb. These all came in the same tomato-based sloppy sauce. The menu also included saltah, the Yemeni national dish, which consists of a mainly vegetable stew topped with a large dollop of helba: a mixture of fenugreek powder and water. This is supposed to be a good appetiser for a ghat-chewing session. One evening when I was having room service on my own, I ordered it, and when the waiter finally understood my accent, he exclaimed, 'Ah! You're going to have Saltah!' in an excited, conspiratorial way. All of these hot dishes came with rice and flatbread. It was best to try to eat some of the flatbread, or at least tear into it, otherwise it kept reappearing, getting tougher by the day. The rice was usually cold and stale, as if it had been cooked several days previously and left for flies to crawl over.

Several young men shared the duties of waiter on the roof terrace. One of them, who served us quite often, was very beautiful. Dressed in a shirt and jeans, he would take the 25 paces or so to the table in a sort of languid sleep-walk. He had soft round cheeks, full lips, and very long dark lashes. He would perform his duties slowly, minimising the effort, not smiling nor making much eye contact: not relating or wanting attention. Then, with unself-conscious indolence, he sashayed the return journey, charmingly swaying.

One evening there was a girls' night out on the terrace. A party of animated young women smoked fragrant hubble-bubbles, laughed and chattered. Their drinks were, of course, non-alcoholic, and they were black-clothed head to foot and fully veiled, but those factors did not inhibit their merry-making. A couple of Saudis were also on the terrace. Jemima explained, 'Saudi men come to Yemen a lot, because they can chew ghat and have prostitutes here.'

Just beyond the next hairpin bend down from the hotel, there was a restaurant by the roadside, with an impressive stone wall and grand door as if it led to a castle. Jemima and Kamil had pointed it out as a good place to eat. Gordon suggested we try it one evening for a change, so we took the risk of walking the short distance. On the way we passed a good number of intoxicated people lying on the verge. When we entered the restaurant, it was not quite what I had imagined. The wall was just a wall. Behind it, a tarpaulin tent was erected over bare earth, with some wobbly tables and chairs. A few Yemenis were dining.

The staff were delighted to see us. The old man in charge insisted we come into the kitchen to choose what to eat, which happened mainly by sign language. Beside the gate was a small gatehouse, with a stone wall and a corrugated iron roof. Inside was the kitchen. A large wok contained old cooking oil, in which sat some meatballs which were probably even older, awaiting their next re-heating. In an ice-box by the wall we were shown some chicken. Some big guavas were proffered for juicing; unwisely I accepted. We selected our options for different sorts of contamination, and in due course our unappetising meals arrived. The guava juice had the texture of thick porridge.

When we were nearly done, there was some sudden shouting, and the gate was flung open. The Yemeni diners vanished into the shadows, knocking over chairs in their haste. A couple of military vehicles with bright headlamps and blaring sirens screeched crazily around the bend and dashed down the hill. The next morning, the Ministry personnel and the hotel manager were elated: there had been a shoot-out and seven senior Al-Qaeda terrorists had been killed; others had got away.

On one of the free days, we went on school visits arranged for us by the local district office, who had also provided interpreters and arranged transport. My visit was to a secondary school higher up the mountain. The cars were amazing: ancient, beaten-up, but able to cope with steep gradients and cart-track surfaces. They shared these punishing tracks with the equally old and dilapidated small yellow Toyota minibuses which provided transport for the locals. After these visits we converged on another school where Gordon and I were to observe a prize-giving and to assist by giving out some of the prizes. It was interesting to see how this celebratory social occasion was organised in such a different cultural context.

On another day, I accompanied Gordon on some sight-seeing, which began with a day-time return visit to the souk. It was still a very interesting experience, and it was nice to actually see things, but there was none of the atmosphere and excitement of the night visit. The sights included great single-item piles of vegetables: onions, chillies, garlic, neatly-stacked mooli and many more; bananas and small sun-dried fish like whitebait. There were many piles of these, and I found their smell appetising: it reminded me of the 'Bombay ducks' that used to be a standard menu item in Indian restaurants before they were banned. Spice stalls had brightly-coloured piled-up bowls of powders and seeds. The local cheeses, another popular item, were flat and round with a brown outer surface. There were sacks and bowls of pulses, and heaps of something that looked like dried seaweed. Gourd containers hung from many stalls; others sold straw hats and basketwork. At a hardware stall, a tool-maker was fitting hafts to hammerheads. The blacksmith was still forging this and that. I was struck by the timelessness of what was going on here in these streets in Ta'iz: it must have been just the same in streets in ancient Rome or Athens.

Next we went to the former palace of the Imam who used to rule Ta'iz, who died in 1962. It was closed for repairs, but we could look around outside. The building was of many storeys: a square stone block in the Yemeni style, with much intricate ornamentation. Inside, everything is preserved as it was at the time of the Imam's death, so that people can see his lifestyle. We had a good view of Cairo Castle: an ancient white sugar-candy fortress covering the top of a high hill, and still in military use. A few days later, Gordon walked up to it one evening with some of the next delegation, but I knew it would have been too strenuous for me.

Finally, we visited the wonderful old Al-Ashrafiyyah Mosque, its bright white minarets making the sky seem deep cobalt blue by comparison. Beyond its grand wooden door, we passed the ablutions area and entered the vast cavernous spaces of the mosque. Much of the stonework was intricately carved. Outside, small goats wandered around while we waited for a taxi.

These diversions notwithstanding, the over-riding quality of my stay in Ta'iz was deadly tedium. I continued to feel ill, weak and listless, having had diarrhoea for a fortnight. I slept poorly. There were long periods in which I had nothing to do except read the two books I had taken with me, and no means of communication with the outside world. For security reasons I did not feel it appropriate to wander around the neighbourhood and spent most of the free time in my room. Its spaciousness was not much compensation. The bath water was brown coloured and very rarely warm. The food, as noted, was unappetising and unvaried. The days were punctuated by the prolonged amplified wail of the call to prayer, and the view from the window by the changing light conditions and the behaviour of the soaring flocks of large crows and kites. I made a chart which I kept on the desk, with boxes for the days until I could go home, and ticked them off as a prisoner might.

When the schedule allowed, Gordon would suggest that we meet on the roof terrace at a certain time to take afternoon tea. I would look forward to these welcome occasions, and it made me feel as if we were like two old men in an old people's home, where a cup of Lipton's Yellow Label and 20 minutes' conversation became an immensely important highlight of the day.

The second delegation arrived and the programme for them started on Sunday. On that same day, to my relief, Jemima and Kamil confirmed our outward flights to prevent the problem I had experienced previously. A Minister turned up to harangue the group. Wearing a pinstripe suit, he strode in with his entourage, completely ignoring myself and my team, and anything we might have been attempting to do. He expressed his opinions exactly as Abdul would have done had he been a Minister rather than a mere Deputy Minister. Shouting, glaring, and thumping the table, he drew the group's attention to the appalling state of education, even here in Ta'iz, 'Our first city'. His talk didn't offer much in the way of solutions.

This group was not quite so diligent as the first: Saalim was not there to keep them in order. They chewed more ghat, took longer breaks and made shorter presentations. On the fieldwork day, I went with a group to an urban school. This was at the 'prison' end of the spectrum: a grim shabby building with no glass in the windows; a boy resignedly holding out his hand to be thrashed with some implement of torture.

We had to fit in a special trip to settle our hotel bills. The manager explained that the credit card machine didn't work, and that the hotel was under the same management as the Sofitel Hotel on the other side of the valley, so we would go there to pay. I was anxious to make sure that this transaction succeeded. Gordon and I set off with the manager on the now familiar route down the mountain and into the centre of Ta'iz. I noticed that where trees or large shrubs bordered the main roads, they were covered with pink and blue fragments of discarded plastic bags. Then we had the new experience of climbing the mountain the other side and getting a new view of the town, and a distant view of our hotel.

The Sofitel was clearly far upmarket from the Jabal Saber. It had luxurious facilities; the credit card machine worked; and it had a gift shop where I bought some trinkets to take home. One of these was an amber and pewter candlestick. On closer examination, the 'amber' looked suspiciously like orange plastic. The Sofitel's large ghat palace was in an interesting style: a modern reproduction of a cross between a castle and a cathedral, built around some large outcrops.

The work finished at the end of Wednesday, and, with relief and delight, at 08.30 on Thursday morning, Gordon and I set off for our 11.30 flight. At one point, when we were away from the town, we had to wait while a herd of camels was led across the road. I enjoyed watching these beautiful animals: some jostled and fretted, some haughtily took their time. The drome was small, with limited facilities. Our first flight was a connection to Sana'a. There were no planes in sight. When one was due, a man walked up and down the runway beating a large clanging drum. I wondered about the significance of this ceremony: Gordon explained it was to get rid of large birds. Our plane, when it came, was a small jet, surprisingly new and luxurious, with rows of two leather seats either side of the gangway. We took off with an amazing surge of power, climbing much more steeply than usual. Much later I learnt that this tactic is popular with pilots who have worked through civil wars.

The airport at Sana'a was familiar ground. We passed through all formalities without problems, and had a long wait in the departure room. 'What nationality do you think they are?' asked Gordon, indicating a middle-aged couple who, despite the heat, were wearing tweeds and carrying Marks and Spencer's bags. The traditionally dressed Yemenis had their jambiyya scabbards empty. We got airborne and I had a happy sense of achievement, or at least, of safe delivery, as we crossed the border into Saudi Arabia, on our way to Bahrain. There, after the privations of Yemen, I was overwhelmed by the glittering opulence of the airport shopping malls, where it seemed that people really do buy diamond-encrusted watches on impulse. We took a deliberate pleasure in choosing to snack in Macdonalds before completing the last leg of the journey, landing at Heathrow on Friday morning.

I had seven weeks in London to do my best to recuperate, tackle the neglected, overdue heaps of the rest of my work, and to prepare for the final phase of the Yemen project, which involved a short session in Sana'a with each of the delegations we had worked with in Ta'iz. There was the by now familiar posturing by the Ministry concerning the composition of our delegation: they liked to make clear their powers in the matter. On this occasion I remained inflexible and took my colleague Anil, who had been included in the original bid without any objection having been raised before now. Anil had a lot of experience and expertise on education within Muslim societies.

We left on a 17.00 flight on Emirates on Friday 22 May. I had arranged to meet Anil at check-in, but was delayed and had to rush to make the flight, and until we were nearly there I did not know whether Anil was on board or not. At Sana'a we were booked into the hotel I had stayed in previously, where I had first met Hassan, which was also to be the training venue.

On Saturday afternoon we got organised, which involved a trip to the Ministry. There were the usual road blocks and gun-toting security forces. One of these road blocks cut off the route we needed to take to the Ministry, and would have required an inconvenient detour. Hassan asked to speak to the officer, and got out to do so. We were allowed through. Back in the car, Hassan told us what the officer had actually said: 'Let them through, they're foreigners: who cares if they get blown up!' In the evening I had a courteous but quite demanding interview with Saalim about the final deliverables for the project. These included a report and resource pack, which became the subject of communications lasting about six months before everything was signed off and the bill for the project paid.

On Sunday and Monday we worked with the first batch of delegates. In the evenings I dined with Anil and much enjoyed his thoughtful conversation, from which among other things I learnt about the Ismaeli sect of Islam to which he belonged. The food was, however, mediocre and I had a kind of intuition that it was not agreeing with me.

The second batch of delegates arrived for the Tuesday and Wednesday sessions, with which Anil coped excellently. I was by now distinctly ill with vomiting and diarrhoea, and so played the minor role. The delegates had been putting into practice working methods they had learnt about previously, and it was pleasantly surprising how positive were some of their reports. The groups also now had a different working culture: less hierarchical, more teamwork and more confidence on the part of the juniors. Abdul was a changed man. His moderate contributions to discussion began with, 'If you please, if I may...' When he arrived he greeted me, beaming, and threw his arms around me. I had no option but to kiss his bristly cheeks. He gave me some special Yemeni bread, which was tough and oily: being near to it made me want to vomit again.

On the last day I drifted minimally through my duties and retired to my room, unable to face anything to eat. A waiter came up with a tray with some yoghurt and a soft drink, which Anil must kindly have arranged, but I couldn't face it and sent him away. My problem was that I could not keep down water and had become significantly dehydrated, having lost so much fluid. Propped up on the bed, my headache was getting worse, my ears were buzzing and I knew I was getting into a potentially tricky condition. The prospect of needing medical assistance was lurking in the shadows, but as an absolutely last resort: I didn't want to get involved with the complications and possible expense, and was very keen to catch my flight in the morning, not least because I was due to set off for China the following week.

I thought some energy would be a good idea. I had some sugar sachets, and opening one, transferred two grains on my finger to my mouth. I didn't vomit, and repeated the process with equal success. Not hurrying, I gradually increased the dosage until the sachet was empty, and then more quickly consumed another. I felt slightly better straight away. I had no bottled water, but there was an apple in the room. I wasn't prepared to eat the peel but by breaking into it, nibbled some of the pulp in very small pieces. That stayed down as well. After about half an hour I felt able to totter down to the bit of the hotel that was open 24 hours to buy a bottle of water, which I took cautiously in tiny sips.

I checked out early next morning. Anil was staying on a few days to do some tourism. President Saleh's official portrait glared sternly down from above the reception desk, as it did over the doorway of every significant building. He was forced from power in 2012, and in 2015 a report to the UN Security Council revealed that he had achieved the premier league of corrupt dictators, having stolen up to $60 billion from his impoverished country. So that is what he was good at. I wondered about the mysterious 'local tax' that had to be top-sliced from the World Bank funding for our project.

I caught the 10.05 flight from Sana'a to Dubai, and arrived at Gatwick at 19.35 the same day. Back in the UK, I found that the trip had impacted adversely on my wealth as well as health. The hotel had charged my credit card twice, once at the hotel, and again at its Omani head office. It took a while for this to show up on my statements, then the credit card company were slow in responding to me. They claimed to have made one 'enquiry' which predictably was ignored, and then eventually told me the matter was time-expired, so I had to bear the loss.

Chapter Eight

I arrived home from Yemen on the evening of Friday 29 May 2009, and was due to fly to China the following Friday, requiring a rapid re-orientation. The project had been in preparation for ages. It involved a group of British international schools in China, branded to a famous independent school in England. The Chinese operation was linked to its 'parent' school in various ways, but was a fully independent company, in effect operating a franchise. Through protracted diplomacy between my organisation and the 'parent' school, and between the 'parent' school and its Chinese offspring, it was established that the Chinese group was interested in buying some services from us.

A meeting was set up to bring the three parties together, completing the triangle. It was hosted by Mary, one of my organisation's top management, in what would normally feel like a capacious conference room. Keeping Mary company were Charlene, Margaret and me. I had met Charlene, who was based in a different part of the organisation, in relation to a consultancy in Kuwait which never happened. They advertised their project; we put in a joint proposal on behalf of our organisation, and it was accepted. Then a problem arose: they didn't realise they would need to pay for it. This wasn't the usual haggling over cost: they had no budget at all and hoped we would do the work as a goodwill gesture. Which we didn't, but in the course of that I got to like Charlene a lot. We worked together on a long-term UK project. She was forthright, could be angular and outrageous, liked a bit of a gossip, and was very clever. Margaret was a member of my headquarters team. She was a seasoned veteran in the provision of short courses in British international schools, travelling often to the Middle East and South East Asia, where she was popular with her regular clients.

A minor commotion announced the arrival of our guests, and a group of at least six or seven men strode into the room. There may have been more: certainly it felt like a dozen or so. Perhaps in reality there were only five, but whatever the number, they filled the room. They all looked the same, even though they were of different heights, widths and ages. The similarity was in their big, boisterous, blokey, self-confident presence; their pinstripe suits, crushing handshakes and noisy introductions; and the military drill with which they marched around the table snapping down business cards. They worked as a tight team, like a rugby side; they were never still, and their mouths were never silent. When not actually talking, all of them continually uttered 'mmm, er, ha ha!' kinds of sounds to maintain their standing in the group dynamic.

After due preliminaries, we got down to business. The outcome was agreement that we should start with a short consultancy visit to scope out in more detail the precise forms of collaboration that would work for both parties. That had been months ago: the detailed arrangements for flights and hotel bookings were finalised while I was travelling back from Yemen. The company had its head office in Shanghai, where we would all start and finish. Its campuses were in Shanghai, Suzhou and Beijing, and we would split up to visit one each. I felt obliged to accept the short straw and go to Beijing. Charlene would go to Suzhou. Margaret was coming to Shanghai directly from a previous engagement in Singapore, and for that reason wanted to stay put in Shanghai. Her flight would land at Shanghai at 6.30 on Saturday 6 June, and she would wait to meet Charlene and me when we landed about 45 minutes later.

Charlene and I set off from Heathrow at 13.00 on Friday, on Virgin, and had a reasonably satisfactory flight. We met up with Margaret and took a taxi to the hotel. Shanghai is an enormous metropolis, rapidly expanding, and overflowing with capital investment. On the ride from the Pudong Airport I felt myself to have shrunk back to child size because everything around was so big. Gigantic tower blocks: new, white, characterless and soulless, grew out of the ground like a pine forest. Big motorways with great big engineered flyovers, cuttings, underpasses and spaghetti junctions swirled between them.

We reached the hotel (a large, new, white tower block) and checked in without problem, remembering to exchange cards in the correct two-handed, bowing posture. The rooms were high grade and very stylish: at least, mine was, I assume the others were the same. It included a glass wall between the ample bathroom and sleeping area, with a blind for guests preferring privacy.

None of us felt a need for an extended period of relaxation, so we arranged to meet up with Frank, our client, at the Shanghai campus which was within walking distance of the hotel. We set off like holiday-makers; Charlene wore a wide-brimmed floppy hat. The whole neighbourhood seemed new and pristine. We walked along a pink pavement the colour of brick-dust, beside a park. The trees and shrubs were mature, so unless they had been planted fully-grown – which you could do with individual plants, but not with a clipped hedge – the newness must have been an optical illusion to some extent. Indeed, there were some older developments, including a large church set in a complex of buildings, like a convent, in a red-brick gothic style.

The school, when we came to it, was set back from the road behind a beautiful green grass playing field. I am sure it was a deliberate design choice to show off this symbol of traditional elite English schooling. The school itself was long and low, mainly two-storey, in a modern style – one has to be practical – but finished in red brick and made to look its part as far as possible. It being Saturday, there were virtually no students present.

We met Frank: he had been one of the party in London. He was the founder and overall big boss of the organisation. We went with him and his wife to a place they knew nearby for a light lunch. It had the feel of a conservatory, and the food was international, not Chinese. I think I had something like a chicken kebab with salad. Fruit juices were a speciality, and, needing to avoid citrus fruit, I had one of beetroot and apple. I don't much like drinking through a straw, which I discarded, but was aware that the froth and fibre were making it a messy business. Just before wiping my face, Frank told me, 'You need to wipe your mouth', as if I was an infant.

Frank was clearly a successful entrepreneur, long-settled in China, but with no previous background in the education sector. Early on it was clear that he felt, far more than he needed to, that he was an amateur in the field; it was equally clear that the school principals were taking advantage of that reticence. Frank explained that concerns about finding suitable schools for their own children had been a factor in starting the business. I could imagine the conversation: 'I'm a bit worried about finding nice schools for our children.' 'OK, darling, I'll build some.'

Back at the hotel, the three of us planned our work and dined together. There was a menu written in English, but nothing so convenient as set meals, and no indication of the sizes of the individual items. This made ordering a bit hit-and-miss: we ended up with quite a bit of food on the table including big piles of sugar snap peas and broccoli, which were very bright green but only luke-warm. Charlene explained that the colour was achieved by running them under a cold tap. My meal included soft-shelled crab: a local speciality which consisted mainly of long, thin legs which were hardly cooked.

From my bedroom window I could see the cathedral, or whatever it was, and white tower blocks stretching into the grey-misted distance. At another angle was a different form of building: lower, longer, with a jagged, fussy style. At first glance I thought it was low-grade tenements, but when I looked more carefully it was new, and meant to be that way: with foresight, the new town included architect-designed future slums.

On Sunday morning Frank arranged for a taxi to take us to his head office in downtown Shanghai. The entrance was near a busy corner: it led to the foyer of an office block with multiple occupants. At the correct floor, quite a way up, we found a suite of several offices and meeting rooms. Frank introduced us to the people who happened to be around, including the Director of Finance, a sharp, eagle-eyed Swiss who was keenly interested in our work.

We also met Henry, a seasoned educational administrator who was leading various projects and developments. I remembered boyhood story books about ships and the sea which included the expression 'old China hands', to describe those who had reliable knowledge of the shoals and currents of the Yellow Sea. Henry was an old China hand in the education business. He knew the country, and how to navigate its Byzantine officialdom. He had roved around, making himself useful. He told us how sometimes he had made the journey from England to Shanghai by train: starting with the boat train across the channel, then linking to the trans-Siberian railway to Vladivostock, from where various links proceeded into China. I think he said it took about two weeks, and he described characters along the way, including the traders who hawked their goods at every station. So that put our tame little trip into its proper perspective.

We talked about what we should particularly look out for at the campuses we were visiting, then Frank took us and his team out to lunch. This involved a brisk walk along the pavement of a busy city-centre street, requiring some attention to the avoidance of collisions. Flocks of starlings at roosting time pass through each other with wonderful precision. I wondered whether a party of Brits among the Shanghai flock were just not tuned into the right wavelength of the intuitive radar needed to achieve the same in a crowd. That apart, there was nothing 'foreign' about the street. In parts of central London there are areas (I don't mean Chinatown) that are sufficiently 'global' that I think they could well be mistaken for part of a city in the Far East. On that walk in Shanghai, I felt I could easily have been in London, except that there was more Chinese writing on display.

The way to the restaurant was up a great flight of steps and into the start of a shopping mall. A table had been reserved large enough for us all to sit around, which automatically limited prospects for conversation. Frank was next to me. I spent much of the meal trying to persuade him to feel more confident about giving leadership on some educational matters on which he had well-considered views. The food was Chinese, and much nicer than my memories of Beijing: dare I say, almost as nice as Chinese food in London.

In the afternoon, Charlene and I checked out of the hotel. She took a scenic train ride to Suzhou. Margaret stayed, to start her work at the Shanghai campus. I took a taxi to the drome to fly to Beijing. It turned out that this allocation of tasks among us happened also, and quite by chance, to match our personalities and profiles to the principals we were visiting.

In my suitcase was a glass bottle containing a mixture that was supposed to cure my sore throat. It was a stupid idea to bring it. At the drome an official – young, slender, but firm – took me to a special room and confronted me with my suitcase, as if expecting me to make a confession. I unpacked the bottle. He took it away, then reappeared and gave it back with an air of serious disapproval. I was the only non-Chinese on the flight. At Beijing, as I was about to leave the baggage hall, I was impressed that an official wanted to see the luggage tag stuck to my boarding pass to make sure it matched the one on my case. Fortunately I hadn't lost it, but this was a new experience. I had thought the tag was to help people find their own luggage. This was reassuring as I often wondered about the likelihood of common styles of cases being wrongly selected.

I met up with Bernard, the principal of the Beijing campus. He took me to dinner with his senior leadership team; he chose a Singapore restaurant, where the food was good. Bernard was experienced: older than me, he had previously directed a group of schools in Hong Kong. The campus in Beijing had incorporated a previous school and had taken a lot of pulling into shape. He knew what he was doing, was relaxed in his role, and clearly saw himself, with justification, as the principal-in-chief of Frank's operation. In his dealings with me he was courteous and professional. He was not going to be caught out obstructing head office's wishes, but at the same time I knew he would make sure that his influence in the company was not going to be limited by consultants from London.

I was accommodated in a hotel near to the school, both being on the fringes of the diplomatic quarter of Beijing, east-north-east of the city centre. Residential districts for ex-pats of various nationalities were in their own separate enclosed compounds, walled around like country estates. The children from these provided the school's main clientele. It was a day-school, offering an education in the elite English tradition, reproducing as nearly as possible the ethos of its English franchisor. Although a recent development, it had the same air of old-fashionedness. As usual among such schools, the English ex-pat teachers were generously rewarded, while the sizeable Chinese staff were on local rates, and also had their own Chinese manager, adding a definite two-tier structure to the traditional hierarchies.

Bernard had everything in apple-pie order. He showed me the outcomes of an American quality assurance scheme he had bought into. He had arranged a schedule of interviews and classroom observations. I worked my way through it. I met the head of the early years unit which had a separate site nearby. We had lunch in the staff canteen which was a pleasant cafeteria in a kind of cedar-wood lodge. All of the people I met were obliging. Some were keen about development; some were defensive.

I was taken for dinner at a Chinese restaurant in the vicinity, which seemed to consist of a series of round thatched huts linked by covered walkways. Near the way in there was an animal enclosure with various edible beasts including a deer with large antlers, presumably being saved up for a special banquet. Around the reception desk and along the main walkway were large earthenware bottles of different shapes and sizes. Bernard explained that they contained different varieties of a kind of local beer that had been aged for a long time and was considered a delicacy.

On Tuesday I had a further schedule of interviews – Bernard worked me pretty hard – then I was driven to the drome to go back to Shanghai. The problem of the glass bottle was repeated. I boarded what must have been one of the oldest Airbuses still flying: its carpets and seats were worn threadbare. Again I was the only non-Chinese. I had the interesting experience of being handed an authentic Chinese in-flight meal in a small cardboard box. By the time I had got back to the same hotel as before, and re-checked in to the same room, I was feeling seriously tired. I texted my wife to let her know I was back and listed tea, tablets and sweets as my immediate agenda.

Charlene and Margaret had finished their work earlier, having been based more locally, and had been out doing something in the town. When they got back, they wanted to meet up so we could compare stories and issues. Not knowing what room I was in, they had asked the staff on reception to phone me. Then, a receptionist having somewhat reluctantly told me there were two women wishing to speak to me, Charlene took the phone and scandalised them by saying, 'Hello darling, can we come up?'

We de-briefed in my room, in the military sense of the word. Margaret had given pastoral and coaching support to the principal in Shanghai, where there had been a succession of numerous principals staying for only short periods. Proximity to head office, and the fact that Frank's children attended the school and his wife took an active interest, may have contributed to that instability. Charlene's school in Suzhou was still at the stage of partial development. It had a young, brash principal whose management style fell short of ideal. 'You haven't got a bloody clue!' Charlene had advised him. Somehow, word had got out there that head office would pick up the expenses charged to Charlene's hotel room, and the school staff had used this knowledge to enjoy a bit of a free drinks party, which may have given Frank a false impression of her lifestyle.

Wednesday was filled with one long meeting in the head office with Frank and the Director of Finance. It was broken into a series of different parts as we worked through issues, and there were periods when we were left on our own to add detail to our proposals. We covered a lot of ground: Frank got his money's worth. At a certain point, a somewhat late lunch appeared: very British filled crusty rolls were bought in so as not to interrupt our productivity.

It was among the most intensive, but also most positive, days of consultancy I could remember. Frank was quick-witted; keen on his own learning and development, and that of his organisation, which gave a sense of genuine engagement. He listened to our reports and judgements with an open yet critical mind. He was also a sharp and successful businessman, not given to acting impulsively or taking unnecessary risks, nor to spending a penny more than necessary. The Director of Finance was the same, as one might expect, but Frank had the better strategic grasp of the education business. We made rec-ommendations for an ongoing relationship, in which we would provide some training in schools, and a range of consultancy support to head office which could be drawn down flexibly. This was agreed in principle, with some enthusiasm on both sides. We would write up our report, and take the discussion to the next stage when Frank and his team visited London in the near future.

Charlene, Margaret and I took an evening stroll and dined in a restaurant a few streets away. It was international rather than Chinese. We ate moderately. Fruit juices were a speciality, but I expected these to be drink rather than food: I asked for a tomato juice, and received a pint tumbler filled with fresh tomatoes chopped not very finely, and hence difficult to eat without a spoon. The return flight the next morning passed uneventfully, and because of the time difference, we landed at Heathrow in the afternoon of the same day, full of positive hopes for the project. Some weeks later we met Frank and his team in London, then did some work by telephone with the school principals. That marked the end of my direct involvement in the project; Margaret and Charlene went back to China to provide some training programmes.

Meanwhile, in the autumn of 2009, I was involved in complex and difficult negotiations regarding a new project in Saudi Arabia. The complexity arose from the number of parties and the power dynamics involved. The Saudi Government had designed an ambitious programme based on the work, ideas, and consultancy support of a British expert, Judith. The job of managing the implementation of the programme had been given to a project management company which had come to an arrangement with Judith, and which wanted my organisation to deliver certain strands of activity. Judith dealt directly with my organisation's top management.

The difficulty arose from the funding on offer being seriously inadequate, and from the terms of the contract being seriously punitive. The more that I raised these concerns, the more Judith airily assured everyone that I was fussing unnecessarily and being an awkward nuisance, and that everything would be fine. These assurances, repeated to me by top managers, that it would be a good thing for our organisation to be involved, and I should be able to sort out the details amicably, were always verbal, not written. The terms of the contract gave the contractor the right unilaterally to define the quantity and quality of our outputs, under pain of financial penalties, in tones implying that for each day's work paid for, we would be lucky to get away with less than three or five. Quite possibly we would have to complete the whole assignment for no pay at all and a high risk of reputational damage. I knew that all the verbal assurances would be forgotten, and I would be held personally accountable for taking my organisation into a bad contract.

Meetings took place with the contractor to try to work through these matters. I say 'the contractor', but actually most of the people we dealt with were freelancers who were themselves between a rock and a hard place: if they started to be too reasonable, they would put their own pay in jeopardy. So we talked about 'working in partnership', but getting the draft contract changed remained elusive. Judith came to a meeting to brief us about the programme, and suggested I might find it helpful to attend a Saudi-based induction activity. I was keen; we looked at dates and diaries. When I followed up that conversation, she sent an e-mail, copied widely, berating me for presuming to think it appropriate for me to 'ask' to be included in the event. In November the contractor invited me to a briefing session at a London address which sounded like an exhibition centre. When I found it, it was someone's private house. When Judith arrived, she greeted me with, 'I didn't know you were going to be here!'

Meanwhile I assembled a team who would write course materials and deliver courses to groups of Saudi school principals and middle managers. This work had to get under way, as the schedule was for our team to set off for Riyadh on 26 February to deliver the first set of activities. All of the parties involved took it as a 'done deal' that we were going to be delivering this programme. That applied to our own activities as much as to anyone else's. The problem was that the deal was still very far from done.

My organisation's contracts experts had been working on modified terms that would more nearly match our normal ways of doing business. Their interactions with the contractor were still inconclusive when activity stopped for the Christmas holidays. Not surprisingly, I couldn't get much response to my continuing representations over the festive period.

It was a welcome distraction to set off for Kuala Lumpur in the first week of January 2010 to attend a conference. This annual mid-winter event, concerning my own field of interest, was hosted by different countries in turn. Before joining my organisation I had spent some years freelancing, and had started going to these conferences then, visiting Toronto, Copenhagen and Rotterdam. As a freelancer I could not afford to attend the conferences held farther afield. My organisation paid for a delegation to attend each year, and the prospect of experiencing Kuala Lumpur was sufficiently attractive to prompt me to write a conference paper.

I flew out on Monday 4 January with a colleague called Tracey. On the descent, Malaya seemed to be covered with densely cultivated trees: a carpet of rich greens. I let Tracey lead the way through the enormous, spanking-new terminal. We took a capacious taxi for the quite lengthy drive to the city centre. The views along this ride suggested enterprise, investment in capital infrastructure, and fertile soils intensively farmed. The city, when we got to it, was amazing: like Singapore, only moreso. Everything screamed modernity and prosperity, including enormous skyscrapers and pleasant parks. We were lodged in the Traders Hotel: a large, funkily modern, very high spec international hotel. From my room on one of the higher floors I had spectacular views of the heart of Kuala Lumpur, looking out over a park and across to the Suria KLCC shopping centre. The famous Petronas Towers were also nearby.

The conference venue was adjacent to the hotel. I took detours through the park. Often the weather seemed to combine sweaty humidity with blazing sun. I soaked in the scene, in both senses. It did not matter that the park was so obviously new and artificial, with tropical plants stuck in among bark chips: this was Kuala Lumpur, and it felt unreal to be walking in this place of historic associations, and modern, in-your-face enterprise and prosperity. One day I walked into the shopping centre, just to see what it was like, but I did not stay long.

Overwhelmingly enormous, the shops were mainly familiar Western outlets. I had no intention of buying anything, and as everyone else was rushing around purposefully, I felt my aimlessness was attracting disapproval.

Numbers varied quite widely at these conferences. When they were held outside North America, very few Americans came. The European ones were more intimate, having almost a family feel. In other global locations a big factor was the level of involvement by the host nation. On this occasion, the Malaysian Ministry of Education had funded a large national delegation, which with the visiting delegations made it feel like a major international conference. Senior experts with global reputations always use the opportunity to hob-nob with each other. I didn't see Tracey the whole week, until we met up for the return taxi ride to the airport on Saturday. Other delegates from my organisation, with one exception, were of top-table calibre, on the conference organising committee, sorting out who would take what position in the coming year, and what books they would write together. On the few occasions I passed them in their august company, it was only natural that they would not bother to acknowledge me.

The exception was a very able, highly educated and thoroughly delightful colleague called Sveta, who combined cutting-edge work with a modest and natural disposition. The topics of our papers were related and we attended each other's sessions. For much of the time I attached myself to a group I knew from a previous organisation I had worked with. I had not seen them for years, and as none of them were 'big names', we could enjoy relaxed sociability.

During breaks most of the delegates milled about in a long, curved corridor with windows on one side, giving good views of the city centre. This was where the bookstalls were located and refreshments served. The Malaysian women wore Muslim-style clothes, but in bright colours: instead of Middle Eastern black, here they made a sea of brilliant rainbow colours and patterns. The host country organisers had made sure we would sample plenty of local delicacies. The mid-morning and mid-afternoon refreshments presented many colourful confections, most of which included various forms of sticky rice, to the extent that after a few days I thought I had better lay off them for the sake of intestinal comfort. Lunch was always a delicious Malaysian hot buffet.

I could not entirely escape the troublesome matter of the contract for the Saudi programme. I am almost ashamed to record that I was still travelling without a laptop, but I had some internet sessions in the hotel's excellent business lounge. The news was not good. A senior manager in the contractor's organisation, who had not been party to the attempts at rapprochement, was taking the sort of belligerent line they would use against a powerless individual freelancer. I felt I had no option but to take a stand to force the parties to negotiate properly. So I told the manager, on behalf of my organisation, that our delegation would not be getting on the plane on 26 February without a contract having been signed that met our requirements, and that in the meantime they had no right to be telling the Saudis or anyone else that they had contracted us to do the work. I knew that this would ruffle feathers, and that I might be unpopular, and those thoughts were uppermost in my mind as I returned to London.

Chapter Nine

Soon after returning from Kuala Lumpur, and while the contract for the Saudi project was still far from resolved, I had the pleasant surprise of an opportunity to go to Saudi Arabia on a different matter. This was a business development trip, funded by my organisation. The itinerary was to take in Jeddah, which I was keen to see, as well as showing presence at a marketing event in Riyadh. Apart from myself, the visiting delegation was to include Gunter who was a senior and highly respected expert; Humphrey who would manage everything, and two female researchers who both had the advantage of being Saudi citizens with useful connections. One was called Fatima, the other, Nadine.

Nadine was quiet and unassuming; I have no particular memory of meeting her before arriving in Jeddah. Fatima was the opposite. Some briefing meetings were organised by senior management, and I first met her in one of those. Fatima was amazing. She was very confident and outgoing; she loved to organise things, to pull strings and make things happen. She was on the fringes of the Saudi royal family, which gave a whole new meaning to 'making things happen'. She spoke, a lot, in a delicious American-Arabian accent, advising on the schedule, reporting things she had set up, briefing us on customs and etiquette.

As before, there was uncertainty about when the Saudi embassy would release the visas, and whether we would be able to collect passports from the visa agency in time to catch the flight. On Thursday 21 January 2010 I set off in a taxi with Humphrey at the end of the day, with the planned intention of calling at the visa agency just before it closed. This was achieved, and the passports had arrived a short time previously. Then we had to rush to Terminal 5 for a 19.00 flight, and only just made it. We arrived in Jeddah on Friday, and were driven in a sumptuous, palatial American taxi to the Jeddah Hilton where we were lodging. Gunter was scheduled to arrive that evening.

The Hilton was stunningly opulent: built around a very tall, triangular central atrium with water features, tall palm trees and every comfort. My room was enormous and lavishly furnished, with a balcony giving a pleasant prospect towards the Red Sea, which was beyond hundreds of amply-proportioned buildings made out of white icing-sugar with pink rooves. I explored the room's various comforts, and how to get access to the balcony. When I did so I found the dust and blast of heat much less attractive than it had looked from inside the room, with its ornate, heavy, metal-framed patio furniture. The room itself had two large beds, voluptuously-draped arrangements of curtains, ample jade green easy chairs, and high-grade wooden furniture and fittings of slightly un-Western design: bow-fronted with octagonal marquetry patterns.

Having some free time, I decided to venture out: I wanted to have a Red Sea experience. Security seemed relaxed: I walked through the eddying gust where cold air met hot, and stepped through and over the Hilton's fortifications, passing a distinctly chunky armoured vehicle on which lounged a drowsy soldier. Remembering the view from the balcony, I followed the slightly tatty pavement – it was dusty and apparently very little used – beside a road leading in the right direction, and shortly came to the seafront, along which ran a major road that I needed to cross. I saw no other pedestrian on the streets during the whole of this short outing, and the environment seemed not really designed for them. Choosing a good spot, I stepped through a shrubbery and crossed the first carriageway, then a more substantial plantation in the centre of the road, and so on, but I sensed that every driver was staring at me for behaving so irregularly. The seafront had an almost deserted promenade, and between that and the sea was a shoreline constructed from large lumps of rock. The sea was pale turquoise-blue, almost the colour of glacier ice where the sun shone through the wave-crests.

All my life, I had associated the words 'Red Sea' with its distinctive shape in atlases. Even when listening to people describing things they had done there, I had always imagined those activities from some kind of aerial perspective which retained the Red Sea shape in the distance as a point of reference. With the rational part of my mind I knew it would not look like that: I saw what I expected to see – sunlit water stretching to the horizon. Yet enjoying the moment required orientation to the atlas: so straight ahead, there is Sudan, slightly to the right, Egypt; and further to the right, there is the Sinai peninsula.

I walked a little way to the left. Tiny, scrawny cats came out from among the boulders: I learnt later why they associated people with food. A man sat on the edge of the promenade, looking out to sea. He was sitting on one half of a neatly folded blanket, on the other half of which stood a tall flask from the top of which hung several tags of Lipton's Yellow Label teabags. He had been looking out to sea, but as I came into view, he hailed me: 'Come, have tea!', smiling and pointing to the blanket and the flask. Not being very sociable, I politely made my excuses about being short of time, but recognised the genuine nature of this hospitality. The man wanted the opportunity for a relaxed conversation in English, which, with the tea, could well have become prolonged. After walking a bit further I headed inland, wrongly assuming that the roads followed a simple grid pattern and that it would be a short and simple walk back to the hotel. I found it eventually, having seen rather more un-scenic pavement than I had intended.

That evening, after over-eating from a buffet which perplexed me as to what not to sample, and when to stop, Nadine came to see me. She found me in the lounge: she wanted to fix up a meeting with her father, whose organisation I would be visiting on Monday. This meeting illustrated how impressionable, yet disorientated, I was to the cultural context. Nadine was in a black abaya and headscarf. So drilled had I been about not shaking hands with women, unless they initiated it, that when Nadine, in a tentative and self-conscious way offered her hand, I became confused and, to my shame, ignored the offer. She raised an eyebrow and shrugged slightly at my perversity.

On Saturday I admired the standard of the breakfast buffet, where the grilled tomatoes were neatly beheaded of their woody bit, inverted and garnished with sprigs of thyme. Fatima breezed into our gathering in the foyer to organise a briefing. We were spending the day at a women's university. First, there was the matter of mobile phones. Having established that we couldn't communicate with each other, she dashed out and bought some cheap phones linked to the local network. 'Where we are going, this may be my only way of communicating with you', she explained. She wanted me to put my SIM card into it but I refused because I did not want to be cut off from any calls coming from London. The phone she gave me was impossible to set up to be usable: the display and instructions were in Arabic only and incomprehensible to me.

Fatima had procured a small minibus with sufficient rows of seats to enable her to sit in a separate row from the men, as required. When we arrived at the university, a lot of polite official greetings took place. The main event for which I had prepared had been variously described in terms of my conducting a 'seminar', or 'masterclass', which I had naively assumed would involve working in an interactive sort of way with a smallish group of people interested in my field. That was allocated two hours in the morning, then in the afternoon Gunter would do the same in his specialist field.

The moment came for Gunter, Humphrey and me to be escorted from the reception room to this event. We were led into a full-size hall and up onto the stage. In the auditorium, about 100 men occupied the first few rows. Behind them was an opaque screen, behind which about 200 women sat ready to listen. This segregation, the numbers present and the formality of the set-up clearly ruled out any meaningful relationship with the group. My heart sank, worried about how to fill the allotted time, and about the sheer boredom for all concerned of my wading through my material, speaking slowly and pausing for line by line translation into Arabic. The extent of the sheer awfulness of this session only became apparent to me afterwards, when it emerged that the interpreter, hidden from view somewhere, had a faulty connection to the sound system. By way of briefing, the interpreter had been provided with my actual presentation material, and also a background reference paper. He or she assumed, quite wrongly, that the background paper must be the text of my speech. So after each of my carefully enunciated sentences, the interpreter read out their version of a sentence from the background paper that bore no relation to what I was saying or to the slides I was showing.

As soon as I decently could, after an hour or so, I opened the session to questions. The men, I later discovered, had been rustled up from among education officials and leaders in the locality for the purpose of providing a respectable audience; many would have been there under sufferance. A few asked questions.

When the men had finished, the women were allowed to ask questions. A female voice from behind the screen started to frame a question, and a sentence or two into that process, most of the men got up and left. I assume that the majority of the female audience would have been the staff and students of the host institution, studying a wide range of subjects, very few of whom would have had knowledge or interest in my field. So the conversation did not last very long, and lunch back in the reception room came as a great relief.

After lunch, I sat in the audience while Gunter performed, which he did very well. I learnt a lot from his session and found it interesting: it was difficult to judge how much of it the audience followed. Towards the end of the afternoon, after tea and diplomatic liaison in the reception room, we were offered a guided tour of the building. A warning had been issued that men would be touring at this time, when female staff and students should have finished for the day and gone. Fatima led us along this corridor and that, explaining high quality facilities and an interesting curriculum including a lot of art, culture, media and business. In one room she said, 'This is where students learn the Koran: at any time there will be a group learning the whole of it by heart – here, have a copy', handing us unused copies of a version the size of a paperback, still wrapped up in cellophane.

The tour proceeded smoothly until we emerged from a lift and went into an art-room, to the sudden blood-curdling sound of a woman shrieking and screaming. I caught a fleeting glimpse of a woman dressed in jeans, a long-sleeved pullover, and with hair hanging loose.

Fleeting, because she dived down to hide behind and under successive pieces of furniture in her passage to the door, shrieking all the while, and made the final dash out of the room with arms flailing, beside herself, making sounds as if she was being murdered. Fatima apologised and said that the woman must have missed the vital communication about the tour. While to our Western eyes decently covered, the woman's reaction was the same as how a Western woman might behave if burst in on by strangers while stark naked.

We were given parting gifts excessive in size, weight and generosity, out of all proportion to the minimal service rendered and, frankly, not very mindful of aircraft baggage arrangements. Mine included, as well as the small Koran and a beautifully bound book of artwork produced by students, a huge and gorgeously gilded version of the Koran in two volumes, in a case, which was as heavy as a substantial briefcase, and a glass object. The top of this was crafted to look like an incense burner but I doubt if it would have had much practical functionality as such. The body of the object was a square-section plinth the size and weight of a dumbbell, inscribed with my name and the date and details of the visit; the whole encased in a bed of ruched ivory silk inside a heavy fitted wooden case with double doors, the case being covered with black velvet. As an artefact both of style and hospitality, it screamed Saudi Arabia: such items must change hands in vast numbers. There were other bits and pieces: a framed certificate, and much printed material about the organisation. Knowing Fatima would be visiting my office in London, I had no alternative but to lug it all home.

That evening I went out with Gunter and Humphrey to the seafront. It came alive after dark. Groups sat around enjoying the evening air – a warm breeze from land to sea. A few had constructed cosy nests for themselves of blankets and rugs, with various forms of lighting, and were playing games or cooking food on stoves or barbecues. The scrawny little cats came for scraps which seemed to be thrown quite generously: more Arabian hospitality.

On Sunday morning, Fatima took us in the minibus on a guided tour of the modern part of the town along the seafront. She had arranged an official tour of the old town for later in the day, to coincide with sunset. We proceeded along the coastal boulevard. Its proper name is Al-Kournaish – The Corniche – which seemed a misnomer because the terrain in this area was flat. Perhaps elsewhere it is cut into a cliff: it runs from the Jeddah seaport for 35 kilometres northwards. The scene was one of spaciousness and modernity. Everything seemed recently built, and designed to look like a seaside resort. Therein lay the oddity: Saudi Arabia does not really do tourism. It did not at that time issue tourist visas: foreign visitors were admitted either for business or pilgrimage, except for a small number of official visitors. Migrant workers do not have the leisure or inclination for lazing by the sea, and cultural and religious customs limit the ways in which Saudi citizens can enjoy such facilities. So the spaciousness felt more like emptiness; additionally, it was January: a sad seaside ghost town.

On the inland side of the boulevard, glimpsed between tall and luxuriant palm trees, high-grade residences were set back behind defensive walls. On the other side, after a stretch of featureless promenade and bright blue sea, there was a mosque, beside a row of tall fountains. The road had extensive spaces as roundabouts or islands between the carriageways, with well-tended lawns and flower beds, and plentiful tall street lamps. Further along, the promenade was punctuated by various facilities: a statuesque Pepsi Cola vending machine; a single-storey structure that might have been a café; an enormous lido with a wave pattern painted along its boundary wall, and bounded on the seaward side by what looked like holiday chalets or up-market beach huts. On foot we ambled by the main hub of the frontage: a man-made spit forming a bay, with hotels and shops on its landward side; we looked across to a pier, which had a dozen or so people at its seaward end. Here, a row of waves some distance offshore suggested a bar or breakwater to create an area of calm shallow water. Elsewhere, waves varied in size according to conditions. In good viewing places I looked through clear water to a bed of pale rocks and seaweed. The Red Sea is unusually clear because so few rivers drain silt into it, and because there is little rainfall. I saw just one operational tourist kiosk, devoid of customers, selling the normal array of highly coloured junk, fluttering in the breeze.

This part of Jeddah doubled up as a sculpture park: everywhere, there seemed to be large, robustly constructed sculptures in the abstracted Islamic taste. Along the promenade there were three nearby in my line of vision. All were of metal skeleton or cobweb type, allowing free passage of coastal breezes. One was like an eccentric Ferris wheel, another like a satellite dish with the addition of brightly coloured vanes; and the third seemed to combine abstract interpretations of fish and scallop shells. In one roundabout was a sculpture of heavy white concrete discs of different sizes, standing on edge with black linking sections, like a giant graduated disc harrow. Another included what looked like a lacework doily made out of thick beige composite, draped over an uneven rock, and surmounted by a frilly necklace of black metal, positioned as if it had been caught by a puff of wind. In a shrubbery between carriageways, a great plinth supported two spiny crab shells standing back to back: one sky blue, the other orange. Along one road, a park of lawns, palm trees and shrubs was bordered by a row of asymmetrical inverted triangles, like bisected arrowheads with tautly curved edges, standing like sentries.

Real sentries were not visible, but must have been numerous in the part of the town where there were official buildings. The traffic was heavier: as in the rest of Saudi Arabia, there was no public transport. Gliding through an underpass, Fatima said that this area had been under water during bad flash-flooding the previous year. 'Many homes were damaged. The King was annoyed that a faulty design by civil engineers should cause such inconvenience to Saudi citizens. He gave each of those affected ...' and she mentioned a sum in riyals that I must have misheard, because it seemed impossibly generous. Quite quickly the density of building thinned, with great expanses of sandy earth, and isolated parades of shops with brightly coloured frontages seemingly standing in the middle of nowhere.

That afternoon I had my meeting with Nadine's father regarding possible links with his organisation, then had a moment of leisure enjoying tea and exquisitely made pastries. With Fatima and Nadine present, it was acceptable for us to sit together in the 'families only' section of the Hilton's lounge, where we relaxed on sumptuous crimson sofas, being waited on by South Asian migrant workers. Fatima was within earshot when she heard my beginner's Arabic for the first time, as I asked for tea (of a waiter for whom Arabic would have been just as foreign): 'He said a whole sentence!' she exclaimed to Nadine in surprise.

At 16.30 we set off for Jeddah old town, where we met up with an official guide, and with Fatima's mother who was joining us for the occasion. The guide was a character: full of himself and his authority. He was in early middle age, smelt of sweat, and had a predatory manner towards attractive young women. He was even thick-skinned enough to try it on a little with Fatima, saying that because he knew her family he could use familiar forms of address. He was dressed in standard male Saudi costume, with the addition of a badge hung around his neck: a post-it sized printed card in a plastic holder, which he flourished frequently as a sign of power. At the start of the trip, we needed to cross a road, and instead of waiting two seconds for a car to pass, as I and I am sure the rest of the party would have been happy to do, the guide strode out in front of it, one hand giving a stop sign, the other holding out the badge, while with an impressively steady nerve he stood stock still, staring fixedly at the driver who had to do an emergency stop, whereupon the guide supervised our crossing in the manner of a school crossing patrol person.

The first site on the tour was the building known as Lawrence of Arabia's house, a municipal museum where that great man lived for a period in 1917 when the building formed part of the British Legation. On the pavement outside, a modern sculpture incorporated a row of three old cannons and neatly cemented piles of cannon-balls. Outside, the building's smooth façade was punctuated by windows covered with dark wooden shutters, with arched tops. A few marble steps led up to the front door which was protected by a decorated portico with an arched central section. The first floor window immediately above this feature projected as a rectangular oriel, its lower edge fringed with wooden fretwork shapes which reminded me of the edges of platform canopies at old British Railways stations.

Inside, the ground floor was laid out as a neat, subtly-lit museum, with informative wall displays written in Arabic. Some sections of wall were covered in smooth modern plaster, and others exposed the original building stone. 'Made of coral!' the guide said. I was sceptical of this description, seeing what I assumed was white highly fossiliferous limestone. Later in a guide book I read that because of the weakness of Red Sea coral as a building material, most buildings of this type in Jeddah date only from the early 20th Century, rise no more than five storeys, and are prone to falling down. So probably these blocks were indeed hacked out of contemporary, unfossilised, reef, of which there are vast expanses nearby, much used to create the landscapes in marine water tropical fish tanks. There was a rectangular central stairwell which offered a giddying upward prospect of rich brown woodwork. Rank upon rank of tall bannisters, newels at each corner that were pillars extending the full height of the building, massive cross-beams, and closely-spaced joists underneath each storey combined in optical jazziness.

Outside, we walked behind the guide towards the heart of the old town, past a row of dress shops with cars parked bumper to kerb in front of them, through a square with palm trees, used mainly as a car park, and into a broad residential street. The buildings each side looked like blocks of apartments. The breadth of the street was slightly reduced by dense bumper to kerb parking on both sides, and it was spanned by a pedestrian footbridge. A broad concrete staircase of monumental proportions rose on each side, and the span was an arc of metal slats with sculptural qualities. Near the bridge there was a modern mosque, with a slender minaret much ornamented in traditional style.

The old town, Al-Balad, held two dominant fascinations: the architectural features of the buildings, and its state of dereliction. The houses were generally four storeys high, and in the Arab tradition were internally facing, presenting their external walls right at the edge of their footprint, creating narrow shady streets between them. The main and very distinctive feature of the external walls was the latticed oriel windows, or mashrabiyyah. These constructions were not present on the ground floor but covered most of the surface area of the walls of the storeys above. They varied in style, degree of ornamentation, and in the extent of current dilapidation. The practical purposes of the mashrabiyyah were to provide air circulation, coolness and privacy, especially for the women. The fretwork provided privacy and ventilation, and earthenware jars of water placed in the bay would cool the incoming air. The houses incorporated various chimney-like design features to get rid of hot air. The ground floors of these houses had only a few windows, generally barricaded with stout shutters, and massive ornamental doors of carved timber.

The seven of us stumped along grubby, uneven alley-ways, too narrow for vehicles; the three visitors in wide-eyed amazement while the guide and the three women walked in front, proudly showing off their heritage. On most houses, the wood from which the mashrabiyyah were made was rusty coloured, like teak. On a sizeable minority, it was finished in varying shades between jade and turquoise, a bit like old metal sheets on church rooves. The more elaborate of these constructions were continuous between storeys, so that the ornamented frieze beneath the bay of one window was linked by panelling to the canopy above the bay below. The open parts of the windows were covered by lattice screens, and in most cases the screen formed an additional further projection beyond the oriel bay in the shape of a balcony. These screens were simply made of diagonal lathes laid over another set of lathes in the opposite diagonal. Other parts of the mashrabbiyah were richly ornamented with mouldings, carvings and fretwork.

A few of the houses were in good condition; some had great sections which had tumbled down, like scenes after an air raid; most were between these extremes. Many of the mashrabbiyah in particular were at drunken angles or had fallen to pieces. Almost all of the houses were either unoccupied, or were squatted in by migrant workers, and those had some of the character of a shanty town, including electric cables trailing from windows and across alleys. The exception was that here and there, especially around the fringes of this district, a modern and functioning shop front had been stuck into the ground floor, its illuminated signage and inte-rior contrasting with the wreckage of the rest of the building. Where vehicles could penetrate, the street scene included cars and utility vehicles some years old, dusty and parked erratically, a general spread of litter, more specific piles of rubbish, and rows of dustbins. Dozens of small bony cats were scavenging everywhere, and especially burrowing into the dustbins. Walking past, there would be a sudden commotion as cats argued over scraps or fought their way out of tangled plastic bags. Some months after our visit, a fire swept through Al-Balad, and the dry old wooden lattice-work reacted like tinder, so we were lucky to see these sights when we did.

The houses in Al-Balad mostly belong to important Saudi families, who abandoned them because of their impracticality for modern living. The families both of Fatima and Nadine had properties here and streets with their family names. In a cleaner and better kept portion of the area, we passed some mature trees which were either ash or some similar species, and came to the largest and best maintained house we had seen, which belonged to Nadine's family. It was unoccupied, but the elaborate woodwork was in beautiful condition. The only signs of neglect were at pavement level, where some patches of paint or plaster skim were missing, and some graffiti had been spray-painted. The entrance was a massive timber double door, in an arched frame of the same material, covered all over with deep-relief carving. Either side of the door were windows in the same style, surmounted by elaborate plaster mouldings. A large ornamented sign beside the door displayed the name of the house, which was Nadine's surname.

The guide led us into the souk and took us down the alley specialising in fabrics. There, we passed hundreds of bolts and drapes of ball-gown materials, glittering under strings of typical street-market lights, which in a society whose women wear only black in public, seemed doubly glamorous. The guide must have been well known: from time to time he had puckish exchanges with stall-holders. With one, he appeared to speak crossly, then he explained to us with a smile, 'I told him I work for the Ministry and for the police, and I said that the sign over his shop was not a good sign, and I would have someone come round to take it down!' Then, looking at his watch, he told us we must hurry: I did not know why.

We arrived at the open space – a wide bit of street rather than a square – in front of the Nasif House, which was of historical importance and currently being developed as a museum. There were shops around, and a massive old tree in the middle, which again looked to me like an ash tree: this was reputed to be the first and oldest tree in Jeddah. The three women in our party had given us permission to include them in photographs, and although the light was starting to fade I took the opportunity to get a picture of myself, in a linen suit, with the three of them in their black abayas, underneath the tree. The guide shepherded us into the building.

With an eye on his watch, he gave only the briefest introduction to the museum's contents – the merest orientation – saying that we would look at them properly later. Early in the house's history, the staircase had been replaced by a lower-gradient camel ramp, for the easier bearing of messages and goods to the upper storeys. Up this ramp we proceeded, glancing briefly at the contents of each floor, until after a final flight of steps we emerged onto the top of the flat roof. This was safely walled, and gave extensive views of Jeddah, and nearer to – the surrounding buildings being not so high – views of a hundred tatty rooftops with their satellite dishes and various metal equipment. Looking down giddily, there were views of courtyards and alleys.

On top of the small stone blockhouse from which we had emerged was a wooden construction. Now leaning with age, it had been substantially built, and was decorated with carving. Instead of glass, the window frames held fine wooden lattices, mostly raised. We had been on the roof just long enough to take in the scene, when from a nearby minaret an amplified call to prayer commenced. A nanosecond later, similar calls started from several other minarets. Within fifteen seconds, the number had risen to dozens; within thirty seconds the amplified calls to prayer were sounding from all of the hundreds of mosques in Jeddah.

The guide and the women excused themselves to attend to their devotions, choosing a spot some distance away. The roof was ideally placed to see the darkening sky and to be bathed in the sound. The three Westerners stood apart from each other, experiencing the spirituality of the moment in our different ways. Each individual call was sung to a beautiful Eastern melody which was haunting and invitational, requiring a conscious act of denial on the part of hearers choosing not to respond. When many calls were combined, near and far in multilayered depth, and carried on and on, the overall sound powerfully witnessed the ancient and enduring culture of the city and nation. The guide came up to me: not now puckish, jokey or seductive, but in earnest.

'The call to prayer never ends', he said. 'Cities further east were finishing as we started; as we finish it starts in Alexandria, and so on, all around the world: a ring of prayer.'

The guide directed Nadine to lead us to the wooden structure: he and Fatima wanted to pray some more. Fatima's mother joined our group. We went up some steps into the summer house, the observatory – I did not know the correct term for the structure. The floor was sloping with age; the end away from the entrance was covered with oriental carpets, and surrounded by low cushions. White sheeting covered the low section of wall between cushions and windows. At the other end was a wooden floor on two levels, with more carpets and cushions.

Set on the floor in the middle of the room was a plastic bag of breads, and a round metal tray with a copper teapot, small glass tumblers, and a disposable plastic cup of sugar. We squatted down and Nadine presided, carefully pouring the tea into glasses, passing them round, opening and distributing the bread. The guide and Fatima joined us. Nadine continued to play the hostess, topping up and offering bread. The tea was not very hot, nor tasted particularly good, and the bread was tough and heavy, like some I had in Yemen. Those shortcomings did not detract from the pleasant surprise of this traditional hospitality. Nor can I remember what we talked about, except that the conversation was relaxed, and flowed until the breeze through the lattices felt cool, and the last of the light faded. A crescent moon stood in a turquoise sky above an orange horizon.

After this soothing Arabian night experience came the anti-climax of having to take an interest in the museum.

The upper floors of the building contained many furnishings and artefacts, especially carpets, cushions, low seats, and furniture of dark wood, ornately and deeply carved in the Arabian style. For all their historic significance, these rooms had a dusty, musty feel: a museum in the process of development, but in the meantime looking almost like an up-market junk shop. The lower floors were in a more completed state, with grander exhibits, proper arrangements, lighting and signage. We had to sit and listen to an illustrated talk by the guide about the history of Jeddah: probably an oft-repeated set piece, some parts of which were mildly interesting.

That concluded the official tour. Next, Fatima, who as well as having a devout and serious interest in Arabian culture also appreciated the finer things of life, took us back into the souk to show us the gold market. The souk was busy at night. We passed by grocery stalls, with neatly filled shelves of coloured packets around the walls, and loose piles of products in front. Our route involved a second look at the fabrics street, then we entered a narrow alley of many small shops, which progressed from silver, to gold plated, to gold, to jewellery. The gold shops had brightly-lit displays of great numbers of rings, chains, bracelets, pendants and other forms of jewellery, much of it of fairly chunky gauge, for customers who did not mind being weighed down by their wealth. I had no idea whether this gold offered good or bad value to Western visitors: none of us had the means or inclination to pursue the question.

Next morning, Monday, I had to give a lecture at the institution owned by Nadine's father. About a hundred people were herded in to form an audience, and I did my best not to bore them too much or for too long. Gunter was not with us, wisely preferring to amuse himself. That evening we were due to catch a flight at 20.45 to Riyadh; we planned to check-in at the drome. As we left the institution, we talked about whether we ought to re-confirm our flights. Fatima and Nadine were going shopping, and Fatima said that she would call in at the airline office, which happened to be nearby, to make sure everything was in order. It was arranged (by Fatima of course) that Humphrey and I would while away some time in a branch of Leaf and Bean, which was in sight of where our driver was parked, and then we would go back to the minibus at an agreed time to wait for the women to return.

I enjoyed a large mug of excellent tea; Humphrey seemed equally content with his coffee. As usual in the afternoon with nothing very pressing to do, I was only just awake. In plenty of time we ambled back to the minibus where I continued to sit in semi-stupor. The women returned with a startling burst of noise and activity. The door was flung open, and Nadine, grinning broadly, climbed into the other end of the seat I was sitting on. Amused by my expression of shock and concern at this illicit act, she pointed at the smoky windows and explained, 'Tinted glass today: no-one can see!'. When moving into position, her abaya briefly exposed a glimpse of the blue jeans she was wearing: a reassuring reminder that this was indeed a colleague from our London office. Meanwhile Fatima, elated and very pleased with herself, reported, 'I've checked us all in and have got all your boarding passes here!' 'But how?' I exclaimed, 'You didn't have our passports...' Without those normally essential items, nor with any authority at all other than her social rank and assertive disposition, she had achieved that impressive feat. Fatima was not coming with us: she was booked on the night flight back to London.

In Riyadh we were lodged at the Sheraton, which was a hive of activity. A major trade fair was taking place, and the world – or at least the sector of it most familiar to me – had congregated in Riyadh. When I had left London, which despite seeming an age ago was only a long week-end previously, there had been no resolution of the problems regarding the contractual conditions for my organisation's involvement in the project for the Saudi Ministry of Education. This raised the question of whether and how much it was right to talk of this project as part of our promotion of our organisation. Fatima was clear that we should be shouting about it; I was concerned that would weaken our negotiating position, so spoke more vaguely about possibilities and discussions. Actually I was quite worried about the chance of uncomfortable encounters if word had spread back to the Ministry about our being 'difficult'.

On Tuesday morning I was sitting with Humphrey and Gunter in one of the crowded lounge areas, my mind on the fact that it was my daughter's 25th birthday, occasioning some exchanges of texts. Gunter and I were scheduled to take turns at speaking to groups of invitees here in the hotel during the day. With a chill of recognition I noticed Judith sitting at a table between us and the door. I should not have been surprised: the chances of bumping into her in Riyadh were actually quite high. Encounter was inevitable: I walked past and we exchanged 'good mornings' with equally cool wariness.

The presentations were repetitious, not very well attended, and generally tedious. There was much courteous exchanging of business cards and pleasantries. This set the pattern for the next few days. By the end of our stay in Riyadh, the conversations had included perhaps ten or a dozen potentially serious business prospects, although in the event nothing came of any of them. A punctuation mark was provided by a female attendee at a seminar at the hotel who berated us for not having requested a special licence, which she believed could have been obtained, for our talks at the exhibition centre to be opened to mixed audiences.

The exhibition centre was a short taxi ride away from the hotel. It was a dramatic and stylish modern building, somewhat in the style of a modern airport terminal. Over 300 organisations had their stalls set out in souk-like lanes; my organisation had a small display patch, being too specialised to attract many relevant enquiries from the droves of people treating the exhibition as a day out. We took turns at staffing the display – it was something to do – and during my stint I had conversations with some very interesting people.

The toilets in the exhibition centre were large but not very well maintained. Gunter complained about the need 'to paddle through piss'. On an early occasion, I nearly made a terrible social error. After washing my hands, I walked towards the door and saw a row of nice red and white towels hanging on a row of hooks. Just in time I spotted some paper towels as well and decided they would be more hygienic. A second later, some Saudis came from the washbasins to reclaim their headgear.

On Wednesday we ran more seminars in the hotel, and in the afternoon I bought some internet time in the business centre so that I could e-mail home. I reported the contrast between the holiday atmosphere of Jeddah and the tedium of Riyadh, with its routine of hotel, work and sleep. I found the Sheraton pretty poor in comparison with the Jeddah Hilton. The breakfast buffet seemed to offer an odd mixture of leftovers from last night's dinner buffet. The toaster was so slow that on the one occasion I used it, by the time I finally got back to my table, my place and the rest of my breakfast had been cleared away. On Thursday our talks were at the exhibition centre, at the end of the day. On Friday and Saturday, instead of the usual breakfast, the hotel offered 'brunch by the pool' as if this was some kind of exciting fun, but in reality a less comfortable, more crowded, skimpier offering.

We had a meeting at the higher education ministry on Saturday morning, which was a nice change of setting and routine. As we came out, we were surprised by a pleasantly different call to prayer in what sounded like a female voice: we realised it must be a young boy. That evening there was an official reception at the exhibition centre. Women greeted attendees with trays of stuffed dates. Gunter left early to get ready for the night flight; Humphrey and I were up early on Sunday to catch the 07.50 flight to Heathrow, humping our excessive piles of official gifts. On the final few metres before stepping into the plane, a security guard asked what was in my biggest package. I explained it was the Holy Koran, whereupon he felt a need to pull it out to look at its gilded glory, tearing it in the process.

Back in the office, I had just under four weeks to finalise everything necessary for the first phase of the Saudi project, and to arrange for two subsequent trips: the first to China and the second to South Sudan, which would run more or less end-to-end. A satisfactory contract for the Saudi project was finally achieved, and the team set off from Heathrow for Riyadh on the evening of Friday 26 February. We were running two different programmes, and each of these needed to have segregated groups, so I needed a team of two men and two women. I took old stalwarts Margaret and Gordon, and two colleagues I had not travelled with before: Jolene and Arthur. I was basically supernumerary but planned to help Arthur with his group.

On Saturday we arrived at a branch of the Holiday Inn which would be both our lodging and work venue. Like many Saudi hotels, the rooms for females were in a separate block on the other side of the road. There was no problem about international females coming to the main hotel lounge area for meetings. Margaret had taken Jolene to a shop in Edgware Road to get her suitably kitted out, but she liked to push the boundaries, for example by wandering around the main lounge with hair uncovered and loose, and abaya half unfastened.

Sunday, Monday and Tuesday were training days. The groups were of different sizes, and the one I was with was somewhat smaller than expected. It transpired that only one of this group was a Saudi – the one in Saudi dress – and that the others were migrant workers from a wide spread of other middle eastern countries. Gordon described his group as being like the League of Nations. By contrast, Jolene and Margaret reported that their groups were predominantly Saudi, as well as being particularly able and keen. That was because education was one of the few professions easily open to Saudi women, and for many of the group, being able to go away unsupervised for a few days on a residential course would have been a rare treat. Margaret liked to tell anecdotes of how well she was getting on socially with her group, and how successfully it was all going, in the course of which she mentioned that the husband of one of her group was ringing up every hour to enquire how she was getting on and whether she was alright. Margaret said that she finally put a stop to it by saying that his calls were interfering with her learning.

The interpreter attached to the group I was with was an interesting young man wavering between two cultures. He was intelligent and highly articulate, and had taken the trouble to read up about the main topic of our work. On the first day he wore Saudi dress and acted with traditional decorum. Thereafter, perhaps because he had seen that the majority of the group were non-Saudi, he appeared in a stylish suit – for a few minutes I didn't recognise him and wondered who he was – and during the off-duty moments talked animatedly about his lifestyle of wild parties and debauchery. 'And I do mean debauchery!' he emphasised, flashing and rolling his eyes.

This being the start of a programme considered prestigious by the Ministry, we were subjected to numerous interruptions and interferences by persons expecting to be treated with extreme deference. These fell into three broad groups. I mentioned earlier the complex procurement arrangements surrounding this project, which produced layer upon layer of consultants and project managers. The consultants were mainly what is described in the trade as 'international resource persons', with various vague hooks into the project, and very articulate on the subject of their own vastly important and superior track records. The Saudis in, or connected with, the Ministry were of two main kinds. High-ranking despots were mainly interested in reminding other Saudis of the pecking order: they would stride in and reduce their inferiors to jelly with ferocious glares or brief cutting comments. The other group were those drawn to flirting with the potential economic advantages of our organisation's brand. In a way I came to regard as distinctively Saudi, they would approach me, all smiles, and after a single sentence of social pleasantry, make vague proposals: 'It is important that you have a company registered here; we could set that up, and then, with our connections with the Ministry....'

By the end of the second day, Monday 1 March, I felt that everything was progressing smoothly. I had no desire to go out anywhere, contenting myself with a stroll up and down the hotel's front garden. It did not take many minutes before I felt I had had enough of the bright sunlight and hot, dusty, slightly stale urban air. This minimal excursion made me think that Riyadh had become slightly more relaxed, and less fortified, since my first visit.

The others were out and about at every opportunity. I was friendly with Jolene, having worked with her closely for a couple of years on projects in London. Once or twice she took the not very proper step of popping into my room to keep me updated with this and that, including the team's leisure activities. Jolene was, among a range of skills, a mistress of the art of using just enough feminine wiles to get her way. I was aware of the strategy, and didn't mind at all. That afternoon she popped in to debate whether to go shopping with Margaret and some of the female participants. The problem being that she didn't have much cash, or a credit card... Of course I wanted her to enjoy the experience and lent her 500 riyals, which she repaid a year or so later following a change in circumstances. I was glad to have missed out on the trip, which seemed to have involved street food in the food court of a shopping mall, and hours of poring over feminine fashions and fabrics. I was glad that I had decided to dine on my own, later, in the hotel.

The downside to this was that the food in the hotel was not particularly good, consisting of a breakfast buffet, and a rest-of-the-day buffet, both unvarying. We had decided that there was no point in having room service for a change, because the staff would almost certainly simply come to this buffet to make up the order. That evening, feeling positive towards the world in general, I asked for the a la carte menu and picked a suitably Arabian item. This had grilled meat, some salad, flatbreads, and an enormous bowl of some kind of yoghurt which tasted peculiar. This disagreed with me, to the extent that the next morning I had to ask Arthur to excuse me from my somewhat superfluous role as his co-tutor.

I spent much of the day in or near to the bathroom. We were leaving on the night flight, which meant a couple of hours of hanging around in the lounge after checking out of our rooms. I had been losing a lot of fluid, and needed to re-visit the main toilet facility next to the lounge. There, as well as losing a great deal more fluid, I achieved the surprising feat of creating such an intensely pungent stench that it set off the smoke alarm, and brought staff running in to investigate. They ran out again pretty quickly. I had to wash my hands six times, thoroughly, to remove taint. Slumped on a sofa, I felt distinctly weary. Jolene later said that she thought I would die because I had turned so white and waxy. I remembered the sugar cure, and gathered up a few sachets from nearby tables, which proved an effective pick-me-up. That was just as well, because I had only half a week to get ready, in every sense, for the next assignment.

Chapter Ten

I stride along one of the long walkways at Heathrow towards the gate, having been absent from the place for a mere three days. Out of the window I see hundreds of standard-sized crates of freight, stacked on metal frameworks with wire mesh sides, and looming behind them the hump-backed bulk of a jumbo jet in Cathay Pacific livery. I wonder if it is the one I will be boarding. A few windows later this seems probable: I get a clearer view of the jet moored at a boarding gangway, being tended by vehicles. The flight is at 11.30 and I am in good time. The start of the day seems a long time ago. Somehow I had forgotten to take into account just what a desolate wasteland early Sunday morning can be in terms of public transport. When I had arrived at my suburban station, there had been no trains, nor any taxis. I was wondering what to do when a man similarly stranded procured a taxi by magic – well, by having phoned for it some time previously – and was happy to share it with me. Conversing during the drive into London, the man explained that he was anxious to get home to Belfast.

I had arranged to meet Margaret at the Terminal Three check-in at 08.30. Then, through into Departures, at Margaret's suggestion we had Eggs Benedict for breakfast in Chez Gerard, which was obviously one of her regular haunts. I did not remember having been there before, but decided that the quality and comfort merited the cost. It was in a quieter mall away from the crowded low-grade facilities of the terminal's central gathering space. Then we went our separate ways for the remainder of the time before boarding.

Now I have a moment to reflect on the nature of this assignment. The British Council, as part of its work to promote British culture and business, had negotiated a system in China for sourcing training for Chinese school principals from UK providers. Some weeks previously, my organisation along with many others was invited to make a general proposal of what we could offer. The proposals which were accepted would go on to an approved pool of suppliers; Chinese authorities would then make their own selection, if any, of what to buy. Proposers who got onto the list would be invited to a 'high profile event' in Guangzhou followed by a marketing opportunity in a different area.

The British Council indicated that the 'maximum acceptable daily fee' would be in the region of a figure exactly half of the minimum that our head of finance set as necessary to cover our costs. This sparked the usual angst and debate between top management keenness to get into this market, and departmental concerns about financial accountability. In the end I decided to put in a proposal but with a price tag double the suggested maximum, in order to keep within our own rules. For half a day or so I got slightly frosty reactions for having 'priced us out of consideration', then, surprisingly rapidly, came the message that our proposal was accepted and we should pack our bags for Guangzhou.

As I have done, with a black tweed suit for formal occasions, as the change from the green one I am wearing, judging that I would rather be too warm than too cold; and the usual medicines and comforts, including a small packed meal of leftovers from home. I might appreciate some sustenance on arrival without getting involved in the expense and complications of hotel meals. I don't rate the chances of winning contracts to be very high, but I am interested in seeing and eating in a different part of China. I understand the main elements of Chinese food in Britain to be essentially Cantonese, so am hoping that by going to Canton I will have better culinary experiences than I had further north.

Jumbo jets being heavy and noisy, the flight has not been particularly restful, but Cathay Pacific has a nice style and standard of service. It is Monday morning; we are making the final descent to Hong Kong. The meals have been very good for economy class. These comprised of lunch and breakfast: a smart move on their part to decide that dinner should be the meal to disappear into the gap between time zones. Hong Kong is shrouded in mist. I badly want to catch sufficient glimpses of it to say to myself that I have 'seen' it, and from these I get the impression of a scenic approach, with hills and a harbour. The plane seems to come in low and straight over the water like a flying boat, and then lands on the pier – well, almost. That at least is a sensible arrangement: I got the impression from old

China hands that before the current airport was built, the approach involved flying along a main street between tall buildings and then taking a sharp right turn.

We are slightly behind schedule; our connecting flight to Guangzhou ('Canton': I like the way that international aviation uses old place names) takes off at 08.30. Disembarking with Margaret, she predicts that this may be a significant problem. I am relieved to see a helpful Cathay Pacific employee shouting and waving a board with our flight to Guangzhou scrawled on it; she gathers us in like an efficient shepherd. Then a mad dash ensues, as the group is led barging through queues and security arrangements, into lifts, along corridors, and, panting and ruffled, into the boarding gate. The group making this rushed transfer is an odd bunch of people, and the haste obviates the need for too much polite conversation. It is odd because a fair proportion of the group are people heading to the same event and who, given the purpose of the trip, are consequently in competition with each other. Some seem to know each other, or know of each other, or despite the adverse conditions have managed very quickly to establish who they are up against. All of this happens with the big, bluff bonhomie of competing salespersons: attributes which do not feature in my repertoire. For a few minutes I am next to a woman who knows my organisation, who introduces herself as the head of a primary school who is attached to one of the delegations. Through the swirl and hubbub I catch glimpses of Margaret networking furiously. With a sense of relief I settle in the calm and orderly haven of the connecting flight.

Later that day I took stock of my circumstances, and high in significance was my sense of appreciation to the British Council for having picked the comfortable Westin Hotel both for the lodging and the event venue. Next was my awareness of having developed an unpleasantly heavy cold somewhere between Riyadh and Guangzhou. My room in the Westin was luxurious and stylish, with sliding panels between bathroom and sleeping quarters. It was a good environment for general recuperation, which included eating the packed meal I had brought from home, having a bath, two mugs of tea, and about three hours' sleep.

I had no idea where the hotel was in relation to the geography of the city: whether, for example, it was anywhere near the mighty Pearl River or other notable landmark, and was not really much wiser by the time I departed. After landing, I had had a very long wait for baggage to appear, and then found the allocated driver. There had been a long taxi ride from the airport in a taxi shared with other delegates. I was next to the woman who had already introduced herself. Some years later I worked on a project in which her school was involved: she had to remind me where we had met. The air had struck cool on landing; the drive was through fog and rain. Those conditions and the company made me decide not to try to take photographs. The city seemed to be enormous and was stuffed full of high-rise developments. Driving into Gangzhou was not noticeably very different from driving into Shanghai. Perhaps here it was denser, busier, more cluttered.

I bought some internet time to e-mail home and to keep in touch with matters back at the office. After this trip,

I would have, once again, only a few days before setting off on a difficult assignment in Africa which was taking a lot of organising. Then, at 18.00 local time I had an informal briefing meeting in the foyer with members of the British Council team who were in charge of this project. This was largely about administrative practicalities. The staff were Chinese women: the key one was Emma, the boss, and her principal assistant was Fay, who was younger and even more orientally petite. They were very business-like on money and contractual matters, but when those things were done with, they were concerned for my entertainment. They offered various possibilities, including museums, shopping, ice-skating and other options all of which I declined, saying I didn't need to do anything apart from the scheduled programme. Fay, who was standing very close to me, looked smilingly up at me with her Siamese-kitten eyes, and asked, 'Is there anything at all I can do to make your evening more enjoyable?' Such charming innocence: I hope she couldn't read thoughts. 'No, I'm just fine, thanks', I reassured her.

Actually there was not much time to fill, because I needed to attend a 'cocktail reception' hosted by the British Council, which began at 19.30, although of course only simple souls like me actually turn up at that time. It was at a nearby hotel, and getting there involved a short walk of about five minutes along a street that could have been in London. The event was in a room of black-walled, spot-lit stylishness. Between making polite conversation with local bigwigs and people who might in a loose sense have regarded themselves as potential clients, I partook of a glass of coconut juice, and a selection of not particularly appetising nibbles.

Most memorable was the cold vegetable tempura, their chilled greasy batter presenting an unusual taste sensation.

When the room was full, and the background noise of voices made it difficult for me to make out many of the words that people might have been saying to me, the meeting was called to order. While the British Council, which exists to promote British culture internationally, is staffed almost entirely by nationals of the country it is working in, the very senior ones, those who are really important, are British, of whom the gentleman now speaking was representative.

Standing under well-positioned spotlights, he was tall, with the kind of fit physique which might result from membership of an expensive gym. He was immaculately tailored, groomed and manicured. His manner, voice and demeanour conveyed status and complete self-assurance: unassailably the queen bee in this room. The smooth, fluent phrases graciously filling the room were in either Mandarin or Cantonese. I could not tell one Chinese language from another, but I assumed Mandarin would have been regarded as more genteel. From the attentive expressions of listeners I assumed the performance was virtuoso. Then, 'For our English-speaking guests..' and what I took to be the same material was repeated in the Queen's English: welcomes, explanations, benedictions. These formalities concluded, someone offered me a top-up of coconut juice, and our host circuited the room: the jolly, avuncular colonial administrator putting his inferiors at ease. Knowing my place, and not in fact feeling particularly at ease (through no-one's fault but my own lack of social skills), I slipped away as soon as appropriate. The cold affected my sinuses and I spent a fair bit of the night awake because of face-ache.

Now it is Tuesday evening, and the first day of the 'high profile event' has been memorable in a range of ways. I am feeling slightly better, but have, nevertheless, been snivelling unattractively over those around me, which is hardly ideal at a marketing event. That notwithstanding, Emma told me a little while ago that we have gained a significant contract with the host province here in Guangdong, where the authorities have been working with a team from another provider (who are here) for the last few years, but want to trade up to a more prestigious organisation. Emma had known this all along: that's why they got us out here.

The event started on the 40th floor, which had windows on all four sides, through which the views composed themselves into two main panoramas: one with hills in the background, so probably towards the north, and the other, in the opposite direction, without. The sky was too overcast for me to get any bearings by looking at shadows.

The southward panorama was dominated by what seemed to be sports facilities and public parks, surrounded by the usual forest of tower blocks. To the right of this scene, the tower block next to the hotel stood on a curved row of shops, the nearest of which was instantly recognisable as a McDonalds burger bar. The words 'McDonalds' and 'I'm lovin' it' were the only non-Chinese script visible. In the middle distance was a row of rectangular open spaces. Starting from the left, the first of these was a modern ornamental garden of trees and walkways in a bold geometric design. Next was a row of brightly surfaced games pitches, then a much larger square of worn-out grass surrounded by maroon surfaces which looked like an old running track, now built over at one end. Some straight tracks and triangular features suggested other forms of athletics, and I could make out the tall poles of floodlights. Over to the right was another old-looking grass surface surrounded by trees. Between these two grass squares a long rectangle of new-looking space was devoted to a prestigious approach to an enormous new sports arena lying behind, and presumably replacing, the facilities described. To the left and right of the arena there were half a dozen buildings which could have been indoor sports arenas of one kind and another. The spaces between and around them were planted quite densely with dark green trees, giving the townscape a damp lush look. To the left of all this ran a great tree-lined boulevard with tower blocks beyond. Straight ahead but more distantly beyond the arena, rose taller tower blocks in a variety of styles, between which I saw the misty but unmistakeable outline of the Guangzhou Tower.

The northern aspect of the panorama did not form such clear patterns. There were a few patches of low-rise residential blocks, of a mere seven or eight storeys; the majority of buildings were twice or three times that height, with a few skyscrapers dotted among them. The nearest skyscraper, of 42 floors, was only half-finished: a glass-less beehive of dull concrete. The hills rising behind the city were lumpy, vegetated, and appeared sage-green through the slight mist.

Crowds milled around and the event got under way. Presentations arranged by the British Council highlighted the marvellous successes of the UK Government's education policies. I wondered if I was the only Brit cringing at this: having my own opinion, being mindful of how deeply contested some of the policy babble is back home, and concerned for the gullibility of the Chinese delegates if they were taking it all at face value. Lunch involved an unseemly scrum to get a small plate of not very exciting finger buffet items. I gave a minor presentation and acted as a panellist. Somewhere else Margaret would have been doing the same: we had separate schedules, which suited us both fine. Simultaneous translation arrangements were in place, with their usual fiddley equipment, and energetic interpreters in stuffy little booths needing to query technical terms.

I really wished I had not attended the last session of the day. Curiosity took me to it, and cowardice kept me there, because walking out would have been such an issue. For the whole of one very long hour, in the main conference hall, 300 delegates were coerced into pretending to be an orchestra. For what reason I can't imagine. The leader of this session divided the group into small sections, each of whom had to learn and practice different sorts of clapping rhythmns and other sorts of thumping sounds. Then, after all that practising, the whole 'orchestra' performed together. Great. Probably the other 299 had a lovely fun time: certainly they presented an impression of jolly jape bonhomie. I would have detested the activity in any circumstances because it involved letting someone control me. To make matters worse, I was in the front row, where I habitually sit, and the composition of the groups required me to be squashed beside and almost under the big body of a man representing the organisation we had just unseated contractually. Perhaps he didn't know yet: he ho-ho'd, beamed and clapped away lustily.

This evening Margaret has gone out with some British Council women to find a nice interesting Chinese restaurant. I have had a room service meal of fish and chips, which in its underdone slobberyness managed to take on a slightly local character. Tomorrow will start off being similar to today, with conference activity again in the morning, and more panel work, which will not require any particular preparation because the local custom is to precede any 'question' with a ten minute lecture. Then I have a 500 mile flight to Fuzhou, the second centre I have been allocated. It is nice that Emma and Fay have decided to attach themselves to me for this trip. Margaret goes off in some other direction.

It was sunny and clear on the way to the drome and I could pay attention to the passing scenes. The trees bordering the main road were big and old, with the bottom metre or so of their trunks painted white to protect them from pests. At a spacious road junction the planted areas were bordered with neat low hedges. A traffic light over the centre of the road was supported by a long horizontal bar attached at its other end to a vertical pole; I could almost feel the pole straining to maintain such an unnatural posture. The cars, coaches and pedestrians had a modern and prosperous look; here and there bicycles and goods tricycles added a traditional note.

Each carriageway of the motorway to the terminal was bounded by a heavy and quite tall concrete barrier.

Traffic was light. Beyond the barriers were long vistas of buildings, trees and hills. The buildings had more variety of style and colour than I had expected: terracotta, cream, grey and pink predominated; one row of blocks each had viridian side walls and pink fronts.

In the opulent comfort of the Fuzhou Shangri-La Hotel, Emma and Fay were once again concerned about my evening's entertainment. They recommended the spa in the hotel. Never having set foot in a spa, I must have conveyed less interest and enthusiasm than they considered natural. They became more persuasive, Fay in particular elaborating in her bright-eyed, smiley way: 'They have different kinds of showers and steam and hot pools, very refreshing. We are going, don't you want to come as well?' Fay's English grammar wasn't perfect: I knew this wasn't quite the invitation it sounded. With the rational part of my mind I knew that there would be separate facilities for men and women. Yet the image she conjured up was so exotically glorious that I succumbed: 'Yes, I'll give it a try'.

This was quite a brave step for me. I had no idea what to expect: how things happen in a spa. I hated being parted from important possessions, normally wearing a jacket at all times stuffed with everything that mattered. I carried no suitable apparel, and remembering showers at school assumed that nudity would be the norm among men. I hoped some others would be there from whom I could take my cue. In shirtsleeves, with only my room key in my pocket, I went exploring, and found the hot, wet, chemical-smelling entrance of the spa, where a man gave me a locker key and a towel. There were a few men here and there, in groups, all Chinese. No-one seemed to be wearing anything, so that was alright.

Being very short-sighted, I have the issue of whether to wear glasses in situations where that might not be considered quite the normal thing to be doing. On this occasion I think I must have kept them on to find my way and read notices, and then held them or put them on the side when I entered a small pool. This was a special very hot mineralised tub which no-one else was using. A notice warned users not to stay in longer than 15 minutes. My own indulgence in this stewed lobster experience was probably less than that. I didn't realize at the time that the normal etiquette was probably to take a shower both before and after using the hot tub. I had done a spa thing: that achievement was enough for now. I couldn't wait to get back to the safe and familiar environment of my room, where of course my precious possessions were exactly as I had left them. I ordered a room service meal: something Western, I think it was burger and chips, which came elegantly presented with a folding table, linen napkins and a lot of fine dining attentive fuss.

Early morning sunlight, with hardly any haze, dramatically lit the panoramic view from my window, which must have been at around the thirtieth storey. Some major tree-lined roads carved the scene into rectangles, edged almost entirely with modern high-rise buildings apparently of good quality and with individuality of design. From my angle of vision I could see that the centre of a rectangle nearby was filled with older development: messier, tattier, but not a slum. Most of the newer buildings had between seven and ten storeys. Some of these blocks were topped with integral curved rooves; some had exposed flat rooves with the usual clutter of small blockhouses and building services;

and on some all of that was covered under separate, open-sided awnings of corrugated material. A minority of the buildings were tall blocks similar in height to my hotel: the six nearby within my view were all of different designs and colours. One, presumably a hotel, had a sign poking up into the sky saying 'Golden Welcomes Group', the only English words I could see. In front of that was a feature I thought at first was a railway station, having six parallel linear canopies joined across by a higher level covered footbridge, but I could see no lines: it was probably a bus station.

After a confusingly classy breakfast buffet experience, I had some work meetings to attend. On the way, in the taxi, Fuzhou seemed to be a city of trailing wires. Telegraph wires and much thicker cabling ran untidily in all directions between poles, forming a dense cobweb just above lorry height. The streets were busy and colourful. The shop fronts in particular presented a blaze of red and yellow, with patches of cyan and magenta, in their own name-boards and displays and in large advertisements higher up. Some had rows of scooters parked in front of them. We passed a square of such shops, which also had stalls under bright canopies, trees and the view of a tall pagoda. The next parade of shops included 'Adidas', 'Goldrooster', and 'Peace'. At the venue I had several sessions in which I was supposed to convince various worthies of Fujian Province, which was not particularly prosperous or advanced, that they would like to buy some services at the top end of the price range. These discussions were conducted with the help of interpreters. Some of them were quite positive, all were interesting to me, and everyone was very courteous. Then attention turned to the important matter of the lunch that our kind provincial hosts were providing to mark the occasion.

Quite a large group were settling themselves around the round table while a woman was asking me what I would like to drink with the meal. I took the question literally, as concerning what I personally would like: that seemed to be the tone and spirit in which the question was put. I prefer to avoid alcohol at lunchtime when working, so asked about fruit juices, explaining that I had to avoid citrus fruit. This conversation required the full focus of my attention, because both parties were making heavy weather of communicating. The woman suggested something I couldn't make out, and kept repeating it: it sounded like 'quor' or 'hong'. Still puzzled, someone found a picture of a corn cob. She was offering me corn juice: something I had never had and was happy to try. It turned out to be a thick confection the colour and texture of custard, served warm in a tall tumbler. It tasted pleasant enough, but perhaps an odd accompaniment to a meal.

This matter having been settled, I could turn my attention back to the room, where an unexpected sight met my eye. Too late to do anything about it, I watched tray-loads of tall tumblers of the yellow gloop being distributed. I had not realized that my personal choice was to be inflicted on everyone else. Politely hiding their disappointment, they had probably been expecting a boozy banquet. At least there were gallons of green tea to comfort everyone.

Meanwhile, food started turning up, dishes being plonked down and removed unexpectedly while one did one's best at conversation. There was a kind of fishy soup served like tea: a pot full of very pretty shells, perhaps abalone, and a small bowl into which to pour the clear liquid in which they were steeping.

One of an extensive sequence of dishes was a bowl of broth-like mixture which, I was told, was a local speciality called 'jump over the wall'. A gentleman on my left explained that there were different theories regarding this name, one being that the dish is so nice that you would be happy to jump over a wall in order to get it. In one dish were what I took to be tiny potatoes the size of petit-pois. Towards the end of the meal came a dove-grey slab of squash.

After lunch Emma and Fay took me on a guided walk around part of Fuzhou, with another woman who played the part of guide and organiser. Her work included the kind service of taking photographs of me standing between Emma and Fay, this way and that: 'No, I need to come this side, the light wasn't quite right in that one'. The area they took me to was a preserved or reconstructed section of town as it might have been a long time ago. This was basically a partly pedestrianised series of streets and alleys with buildings in antique style, with explanatory plaques and a lot of sculptures, mainly of life-sized figures representing some of the occupations of days gone by. Just as with the section of the Great Wall I had visited, I did wonder at the time how much of it was of genuine antiquity. Much later, and having looked in guide books, I concluded that the answer was probably none.

It was, nevertheless, a pleasant and interesting walk in the company of three agreeable young women. The buildings were mainly of two storeys. Some were constructed of stone or bricks, the latter ranging from ash grey to brick-red, with elements of ornate timberwork. These included windows that looked like doors, with a top half of glazed panels, and a bottom half of plain wooden panels. Further along the road, the proportion of all-timber buildings increased. The wood was of a dark reddish shade, and included carved panels and windows made of many small panes. With one notable exception, the upper storey did not overhang. Some variations on the theme included sections finished in weatherboarding and similarly homely techniques, like high-class summer-houses. Street lamps were decorated, and the pedestrianised section was furnished with rows of benches and kiosks.

A woman was selling pineapples from a barrow made out of wooden slats and a pair of bicycle wheels. Some of the pineapples were in their natural form, while others had been peeled with neatly intersecting spirals to remove the fibrous bits. Knife in hand, the woman was gradually increasing the peeled proportion. Despite the chilly weather and the absence of any other westerner, the area managed to create a slightly touristy feel.

Some of the buildings were shops selling carved soapstone, this being a local speciality. The shops sold multicoloured beads and lumps in various carved forms, some of which reminded me of plastic replicas of internal organs. There was also a small museum exhibiting more major or historic pieces. These carvings were surprisingly large, intricate and colourful, incorporating the bands of natural colouring in the stone into the composition. One was, I think, depicting a piece of coral reef incorporating sea anemones and other intricate forms, using dark green, white and rust-coloured sections of the stone to distinguish different features. Another was a massive depiction of a willow pattern landscape with figures, using a stone with concentric layers of colour, carved away in the style of a cameo brooch. One depicted corals and seaweeds carved with extreme intricacy using bands of yellow, cream, red and grey stone. There was an angry-looking polar bear with realistic white fur. One carving, in the shape of a great crescent moon of pale green, depicted a fleet of small sailing boats discharging soldiers with ferocious demeanour into waves and up a beach.

The drive back to Fuzhou airport started in daylight; dusk fell along the way, and sightseeing was further impeded by the very dark blue tinting on the taxi windows. The landscape was hilly and the route included the scenic crossing of a great river, Min Jiang. To my right the view was like a watercolour painting using washes of three intensities of Prussian blue. The sky was palest, next in the mid-range were distant mountains and the river itself. In the darkest tone were nearby hills on either bank, linked by a bridge of long low spans, and various boats and small merchant vessels. The overall effect reminded me of some silhouetted views of Eileen Donan Castle.

Back at Guangzhou, I spent a bit of time on Friday morning sending e-mails to my organisation about all the things that now had to be done. Later I began the homeward journey, and it had been arranged that I would go to Hong Kong by train rather than plane, which added a new experience. Having made my way to the enormous atrium of the central station, I was a bit surprised to find that the part of it where I needed to go was an international border. I had not found time to read up in advance about the places I was visiting. I had clear memories of Britain having given Hong Kong back to China in 1997 and had assumed that thirteen years later there would not be much of a border left between them.

The train journey was interesting but views were limited first by fog, and then by nightfall. At Hong Kong an international border was fully in operation. I queued up and got a stamp in my passport saying I was an immigrant entitled to stay for 180 days, followed by a stamp saying 'departed': the shortest visit I could remember making to a jurisdiction, apart perhaps from passing through Luxembourg in my youth. I found a taxi, and was surprised that it drove on the left, and that the roads were still marked out with British road-signs. We crossed a shopping street that looked very much like Oxford Street. At the end of the journey, the taxi driver asked for a sum of money in Hong Kong dollars, a currency I had not known existed. I offered the choice of the only two currencies I had: British and Chinese; he crossly accepted one, I can't remember which, but it was probably inflated in the conversion. The cavernous space of the airport was made less boring than most by a replica of an early flying machine, of Wright Brothers style, suspended from the ceiling. I filled in some of the wait until my 01.00 flight by enjoying a very British meal in a nice restaurant.

Chapter Eleven

I got back from Hong Kong on Saturday. On Monday I had a travel clinic appointment followed by office meetings on other projects, which continued more or less without break throughout Tuesday 16 March, until a point in the afternoon when it was time for me to go to Heathrow Terminal 4 to catch a 19.00 flight to Nairobi, on my way to Southern Sudan.

At that time, in the Spring of 2010, there were still a few years to go before the breakaway territory of Southern Sudan achieved independence as the new country, South Sudan. This raised the question of how best to get into the country. I had only one passport, and the pattern of travel I have been describing, with limited time between trips, meant that being without my passport for the purpose of obtaining new visas had to be very tightly scheduled. Indeed, it was this sequence of trips which prompted me to obtain a second passport, which happened some months later. The very officially proper approach, which my organisation would naturally have gravitated towards, would have been to engage in the

Byzantine process of obtaining permission from the Government of Sudan to enter that country and to pass into its southern rebel territory, which given the length and destructiveness of the civil war would not have been straightforward. Fortunately the practicalities of the situation led to agreement that I should travel to Kenya as a tourist, where there was a system for getting permission from the rebel regime to enter its territory.

The cabin of the Kenyan Airways plane, my first experience of an African airline, seemed warm and good-naturedly busy. The welcoming staff wore a lot of bright red and smelt faintly of sweat. It would be fourteen days before I got back to Heathrow, which I had known all along would be far more days of fieldwork than I needed to do the task. I was to advise on setting up a South Sudan Institute of Education. My client and hosting organisation was UNICEF who had a general co-ordinating role with other aid agencies and with GOSS – the Government of Southern Sudan. The assignment had been brokered by the British Council who were paying my organisation a small allowance for my time: this had all been negotiated with Mary, our senior manager. This payment was way below our true costs, and I agreed with Mary that as I expected to have a lot of hanging around time, I would take a writing assignment for another client, which I could do anywhere, to fill in the spaces and balance the books. I was keen to have this African adventure.

Nine hours of night flight and a three-hour time difference meant that it was bright morning when I landed in Nairobi. I queued up and bought a tourist visa, then took one of the bright yellow taxis lined up outside the drome, to the Intercontinental Hotel. The sky was about three-quarters covered with leaden cloud, through which the sun shone on a mass of tall flagpoles and neatly kept gardens. Spatters of rain fell as the taxi joined the main road to the city, past flat brown savannah and dark green vegetation, including the flat parasols of what I assumed to be acacia trees. I had not reckoned on rain when selecting my clothes. The clouds cleared to show steely blue sky, and the proportion of green to brown on the ground surface seemed to increase, helped by bright green grass verges. Buildings and people appeared: a lot of people were walking to work or school along the six-lane highway. The carriageways were separated by a strip of red-tinged earth with scrubby grass and bushes. Lusher and more extensive vegetation bordered the road to the left (Kenya drives on the left); over on the right I could see warehouses or factories, and a petrol station.

Soon a more mixed urban landscape appeared: a library, a school, rows of single-storey buildings, and a scattering of higher-rise residential blocks. Traffic thickened – mainly cars and light commercial vehicles – and the taxi entered the centre of Nairobi. I had a good view of the parliament building behind its neat iron railings before arriving at the hotel, which was just around the corner in City Hall Way.

During my stay in Nairobi I was to have meetings with two people with whom I had been in e-mail contact. One was Xavier, who worked for the British Council and had set up this assignment; he was my client. The other was a freelance consultant with experience of working in both halves of Sudan, selected by Xavier to undertake a parallel assignment. She was called Nellie, and was a specialist in teaching English. She would have her own work to do but with her local knowledge she would, supposedly, be a reassuring and supportive colleague. Xavier's contacts with my organisation had been extensive, to set up all the practicalities for the trip. E-mail exchanges with Nellie to which I had been copied in had been limited to making sure we would be in the same hotel at the same time in Nairobi, but these had also imparted that Nellie attached great importance to our being accommodated at the best hotel when we got to Juba. I had telephoned her before setting off for China. Our brief conversation informed me that she lived in the south of France and only worked for half of the year; in a spirit of friendliness I told her that I had not been to Africa before – a fact which would need to be shared sooner or later.

Now, at an appointed time, I looked around the plush ambience of the Intercontinental's foyer and bar area wondering if one of the women present was Nellie. An attractive youngish woman of Asian appearance seemed to be waiting to meet someone. With hopefulness, but not much expectation, I asked, 'Excuse me, are you Nellie?' She very pleasantly told me she was not. A white woman of indeterminate age was slouched on a bar stool; I made my enquiry again, this time successfully. I received an empty smile in a face otherwise etched into lines of vinegary resentment, above a body of wobbly obesity. Nellie toppled down from the stool and suggested we find somewhere more comfortable to sit. There, she opined that she just couldn't believe my organisation would send someone who had not been to Africa before. She hoped my advice and report would emphasise the very great importance of her field of work, teaching English; in the course of this she displayed minimal grasp of my own areas of expertise or the point of the assignment. Thus our working relationship got off to a pretty bad start, and while it didn't actually deteriorate, nothing happened to change those first impressions. Later I had a similarly brief, but rather more business-like, introductory meeting with Xavier.

Although the hotel was housed in a modern tower block, its designer had worked hard to create a traditional colonial feel. This was especially evident on the ground floor, where the foyer featured massive buff pillars arranged in an oval. A darkly panelled corridor led to the restaurant, where I enjoyed Nile Perch, and, later, beef stew with plantains, being determined to take advantage of the local flavours, washed down with the local brand of Kenyan tea. Fortunately Nellie showed no inclination to socialise: I don't think we voluntarily had a single meal together during the whole of the assignment, but only on the few occasions when our hosts provided something during working sessions.

My room was just a floor or two up from the public areas, with a good view of central Nairobi, within which particular vista were some tower blocks, car parks, green spaces and tree-lined roads: everything well spread out. The room had a ceramic tiled floor with a rug, floor-to-ceiling windows, a desk, a capacious settee with big floppy cushions, all covered in African-style multi-coloured fabric, and a big ceramic bedside lamp painted to look like tiger skin. A picture of distant lilac mountains rising above peachy savannah completed this pleasant ambience.

That first day I felt tired, and spent periods half asleep and half awake, doing neither thing very well. The causes certainly included the malaria tablets I was taking – for the first and last time: on future travels I judged it better not to bother with them. Remembering how I had felt at Ta'iz, they may also have included the altitude, Nairobi being 5000 feet above sea level. Nellie, making some slight effort to educate or frighten me, had grossly exaggerated this altitude, and the temperatures we would be encountering when we went north. She didn't know that I had been a geography teacher.

When I did drift into a genuinely restful sleep, I was rudely awakened by my mobile phone ringing. A quirk of that phone was that it would receive incoming calls in places where it would not allow outgoing calls. I answered it before realising that I was still half asleep and only very slowly surfacing. Slowly I realised that it was from a work contact who (before this call) was slightly prickly, feeling ill-used, and needed smoothing, cultivating, charming. He would have assumed I was alert and in my office in London. Instead of which I made a fool of myself stammering incoherently and not very helpfully, at such length that the call used up a fair bit of credit.

The bathroom had some minor imperfections. When a power cut occurred while I was using the shower, I found it to be disorientatingly dark. The washbasin plughole fitting was absent, presenting an unappetising view down the dirty drainpipe. The bath did not have a plug. Using that means of entry, a cockroach came to visit me. It was a fine large specimen, very prettily coloured, and waving its long antennae in greeting. I killed it, and asked room service to bring me a bath plug. The man who came hadn't heard clearly, and offered an assortment of other things; shower cap, soap and so on. I explained and eventually he brought one that was almost serviceable. I had acquired a travel plug, and can't think now why I didn't have it with me.

On Thursday, Nellie escorted me in a taxi to the British Council's Nairobi headquarters, where she had business to conduct, and I could meet some people, and we could discuss arrangements with Xavier more formally. Along the way, the impression from my hotel window was confirmed and magnified: broad streets edged with attractive gardens, all well maintained; good quality buildings, and direction signs at some junctions like those that used to adorn country lanes, with place names written on the pointing arms. Trees were luxuriant and numerous, and the soil, wherever it was exposed, was Indian Red.

Nearer to our destination, the scene became more mixed, with areas of hummocky waste-ground, covered in rough grass with patches of building rubble, and some residential tower blocks of less salubrious appearance. The amount of cloud cover had decreased as the morning advanced: now the sun was bright and shadows dark. There were security blocks to steer between and around, and at this point the tarmac or asphalte road surface seemed like a thinly-spread and irregularly-edged layer of icing over the red earth. The British Council building was large and spacious, with rooms a bit like school classrooms, and displays of various projects. It was surrounded by tree-filled gardens and a car park, which as well as the canopy of trees, had canopies of green fabric stretched over curved metal frames to protect the cars from sun and rain. I was introduced to some people who knew about my organisation's involvements in their various different projects, and they gave us a light lunch in the canteen. We also met and had a planning meeting with Xavier, who came back to the hotel with us afterwards.

Towards the end of this visit, Nellie asked me to absent myself, because she needed to discuss 'a *professional* matter', giving the word special emphasis. Of course I did so, using the time to admire the carpark. The word has various usages: after a few minutes I realised she was haggling over some payment to which she believed she was entitled. As the taxi drew away from the building, we passed a broad unmetalled track of hummocky red earth, between trees with massive trunks, which cast mottled shade. It was deserted until some distance away where cars were parked at drunken angles and people milled about. The route took us past a public open space, the Uhuru Park Recreation Ground, according to the City Council of Nairobi's sign. The trees around its edge were a type of palm with a very tall spindly trunk topped by a tiny feather duster of foliage.

On the way back in the car, Xavier and Nellie were discussing something within their own field of interest; I was sitting in front, only half listening. 'Oh, he's still in a state of culture shock!' Nellie proclaimed in a satisfied tone, which annoyed me on two counts. It wasn't true, but as I reflected, I couldn't even think what the words actually meant in relation to what we were doing. Staying in an international grade hotel, being driven around central Nairobi, having professional (in the normal sense of the word) meetings: what on earth was I supposed to find culturally shocking? 'You *are* on malaria tablets, aren't you?' she persisted, in a tone with which some people regulate naughty infants. Then, 'Which ones?' I named the more expensive and least harmful of the popular varieties, and Nellie's grunt seemed to acknowledge that she could not reasonably criticise that choice.

Xavier took our passports and said that he would sort out our travel papers: there was no need for us to attend in person. Thus I acquired a beautiful document, a single A5 sheet of card printed front and back which in style was a cross between a passport and a visa. The heading, 'Government of Southern Sudan, Ministry of Internal Affairs, Travel Permit, by authority of the GOSS' sat between a crest and a flag, above my photograph, personal details and travel intentions, stamped front and back, issued by the Nairobi Liaison Office, and shouting to anyone who might view it, 'Look, we are a country, doing proper country border control'.

I had no plans or desire to wander around Nairobi, where there was a lot of street robbery, but thought there was no reason not to amble around the corner to take a better look at the parliament buildings. The massive stone walls either side of its main entrance, which was not visibly fortified, were decorated with deep-relief carvings which combined traditional African motifs in a modern style. Small groups of Kenyan men in shirtsleeves stood around. Returning to the hotel entrance I realised that my Swiss Army knife was in my suit pocket. I couldn't remember why I had needed to unpack it, and decided to try to bluff my way through the security gate. Keeping my jacket on, when the alarm sounded, I smilingly said, 'Look, I've got metal all over me: keys, coins, pens, camera..', showing these various harmless things, 'Do you want me to turn it all out?' The guard let me through.

At the end of our first meeting, Xavier had recommended the Turkish bath in the hotel. Emboldened by my hot dip experience in Fuzhou, I ventured in. Having exchanged my clothes for a towel, I entered a hot, humid room with a row of couches. On the nearest one, an enormous black man lay naked, on his side, his back towards me. At the sound of my entry he turned his head just enough to see who had come in: his expression was inscrutable. A few other men were sitting or reclining further away. I walked through into an inner area which, among other things, included a steam room, which I entered. It was unoccupied: a large cubicle, or small room, with a wooden chair, filled with a thick fog of very hot menthol-smelling vapour. This was a pleasant and cleansing experience. I could see the point of it, feeling every skin pore opening, and, unlike a hot bath, it could not easily be replicated at home. I stood, I sat, I breathed deeply for as long as I could, until my eyes stung and I reached the 'Right, done that now!' stage. Dressed and back in my room, away from the heat and in normal air, I wasn't sure that the steam had produced much noticeable benefit.

On the morning of Friday 19 March, after a short night spoilt by acid reflux and an 03.30 alarm, I arrived with Nellie at the airport at the time we had been told was necessary, and then had to wait an hour before the check-in opened. Eventually we boarded the small plane for the 07.30 flight to Juba, which took just under two hours. On the runway, the scene was of flat yellowish-green fields under a sky of cerulean blue; low-angled morning sunlight shone on bright white patches of air-field buildings scattered along a false horizon. Beyond, but almost obscured by haze, were some mountains.

Soon after take-off, a tract of land-use looked as if a fleet of flying saucers had landed: twenty or so similar-sized circular patches of darker and browner hue suggested circles of cultivation in the surrounding grassland and scrub. Later, a similar pattern comprised different elements: the 'flying saucers' seemed to be pasture-covered clearings in surroundings of dense, dark green forest. On lower ground were grass fields of sharp-edged polygons, linked to each other by arrow-straight tracks. A river had cut a floodplain, which had semi-circular green fields inside each meander.

The small plane flew low enough to give good views of settlements, which were low-density and widely dispersed either side of broad straight roads. Rooves were blue (the colour of plastic sheets), pink and white. One settlement had a nucleus of what could have been industrial and commercial buildings. This was surrounded by perhaps two hundred scattered dwellings, with unclear boundaries, and not arranged along roads but linked by a faint random web of rough earth tracks. Another settlement seemed to lack a nucleus but displayed an orderly grid pattern. Most of its houses occupied clear square plots edged with hedges or walls.

Then an upland landscape appeared with an extraordinary pattern of relief: a tight mesh of valleys deeply etched into blue-green vegetated hills. It was like looking into a rock-pool, like the surface of a brain; in places like a slithering mass of newly-hatched crocodiles. Dropping slightly in altitude, the plane passed part of a large lake or reservoir with a small wooded island, and here the surrounding landscape resolved itself into farmed and lushly vegetated ridges and valleys, with villages at the valley mouths and individual buildings scattered along the ridges. What I supposed to be the Rift Valley appeared. Flat farmland was separated by a straight-running fault-line from barren uplands, which formed a dry-looking plateau dissected by ravines. Down on the plain, another lake appeared, and then another surrounded by hillier ground.

The landscape changed to rough savannah, tinged green, ochre and purple, with hummocky hills surrounded by mist: we were in Sudan. Through increasingly grey mist, I had my first view of the Nile, snaking its way across a flat plain, with numerous small islands mid-stream, covered with bushes. The pilot took the plane into a very steep descent, describing a tight spiral: a manoeuvre I later learnt had been developed during the civil war to present a harder target to missiles. The Nile spread its banks here, with several larger islands mid-stream forming a braided channel. I could see the airstrip, and the vast dense sprawl of Juba. The vegetation along the river banks was bright emerald green; further back, where soil was exposed, its colour was raw sienna.

Landing coincided with a rain shower. I splashed uncomfortably through puddles of red mud to the small drome building, which was crowded and seemed to be in a state of chaos. Big men in military uniforms (camouflage battledress, not Number Threes or barrack dress as at normal airports) marshalled people this way and that. My travel papers were inspected and stamped. Baggage arrived and had to be given a chalk mark. A man from UNICEF, seeing two white faces, approached us and said he was to meet two consultants. We gave our names and he seemed to think we were the right people. Nellie and I splashed through more mud to a UNICEF 4x4 vehicle, and the man set off.

Nellie expected that we were being taken to the Lugali House Hotel, having previously made it clear to Xavier that it would be beneath her dignity to stay anywhere else. Knowing the place, she was puzzled by the route and questioned the driver, who explained that he was to deliver us to the television studio for an interview. We were put out that we were expected to do this before having any briefing. At the studio the man left us in the jeep while he went to check arrangements. To make conversation, I said it had been good to see the River Nile. Nellie said that it was quite nice to see it close up: there were good places on the bank. 'We'll have to arrange a trip for you', she offered reluctantly. It never happened. The man came back and said that we were the wrong consultants, and that he would drive us to UNICEF headquarters.

The journey was over very bumpy mud roads. The bumps were large and smooth: a heaving sea of waves and troughs, on which the jeep pitched and rolled. Here and there, sited apparently randomly on patches of waste ground, were round huts with mud walls and conical thatched rooves. Some listed drunkenly; some were falling to pieces. A properly surfaced road appeared, with tree-lined walkways ('pavements' would be an overstatement), boundary walls shielding buildings, and an assortment of cars, motorbikes and pedestrians.

The UNICEF headquarters compound was just off the main road, beyond a patch of rough-surfaced ground that served as a general parking area. The way in was through a secure door in a solid surrounding barricade. Inside, past the guardhouse, the headquarters comprised a series of huts linked by raised wooden walkways with thatched rooves, surrounded by vegetation which reminded me of the hothouses at Kew Gardens. The key personnel connected to our projects were Charles, Simon and Bernard. They came to meet us and Simon took Nellie's large case. Bernard insisted on taking mine, despite my protests. 'I am very happy to wheel your bag: I have one the same, only smaller', he explained. Actually he had made the better choice. Thinking I ought to buy some new luggage suitable for longer trips, I had chosen it having seen the inexpensive but beautifully padded-out display model in the shop. 'One of those, Sir? Fine!', the assistant had said, passing me a thin package wrapped up in polythene. 'Yes it's the same model' he assured me, as indeed it was: a light metal frame with wheels, carrying a flimsy but very capacious bag. The problem was that my luggage made it about two-thirds full, so however carefully I packed, everything slumped to a disordered bulge at the lower end. We went into the meeting hut, where they explained that they had not been expecting us so soon (why not? They had had our flight details some weeks previously). They could not put us into the hotel they had planned because its security rating had been downgraded. Nor could they put us in Lugali House because they had just checked and it was now fully booked. So they were just sorting out an alternative.

Nellie thought that in the meantime it would be a good idea to say hello to the local representatives of the British Council and the Consulate, whose office was just behind Lugali House. A driver was allocated and off we went. Lugali House had a breeze-block security wall and heavy gates of green-painted metal. The breeze-blocks on either side of the gates had been rendered for a section of about one metre, surmounted by stone balls, and painted white, to be in keeping with the house, which was also white, substantial, and of colonial appearance: I could see that Nellie would feel at home here. She led the way to a small office behind the hotel, styled 'Havana House', which housed two desks: one was the British Consulate, the other the local office of the British Council. Only one man was in occupation, I forget which, but he seemed put out to have his peace interrupted by Nellie's grand entrance.

Over the next few days it became clear to me that Juba was thickly populated with international aid agencies, charities and consultants, generally falling over each other in their desire to make a positive contribution, so the arrival of two more was not really headline news. 'We have *arrived*', Nellie explained, as if her corporeal presence might be in doubt, 'So I thought we should report to you and let you know we are here.' With a marked lack of effusion, the man replied, 'Well, if it's the tracker service you are wanting, you do all that on the FCO's website these days: that's been the system for some years now. But nice to see you', he added insincerely, turning attention pointedly back to his desk. When giving instructions to the driver, Nellie had assumed a gracious social call of some duration. Thus dismissed, we had time to spare, and went into the hotel to use the toilets and to have a drink.

The hotel was not much bigger than a large domestic house. Like other hotels in Juba, additional cheaper accommodation was offered in the form of metal containers in the grounds. The hall, toilets and main eating area were paved with cool, rough-hewn stone flags. In the restaurant, the day's menu was chalked on a school blackboard and easel. The tables and chairs were of solid, homely plain wood. I could see that the place had its attractions, but without elegance or opulence: the ambience was like a plain but respectable old country pub. Nellie mellowed into a state nearer to contentment, being in her favourite place, and her taste and judgement being so obviously unquestionable.

The due time elapsed and we walked out to find the driver. He was not there. We went back inside. Nellie had a phone which worked, and phoned UNICEF, to what effect I could not tell. We looked again, and found the vehicle but no driver. After hanging around it for a while, the driver appeared. Nellie berated him. At one point in this lecture, she emphasised that his lateness wasn't just causing inconvenience, but far worse than that, he had 'Made us waste 20 minutes of *valuable consultancy time.*' I doubted whether the driver prized that commodity, and wondered what Nellie believed she might otherwise have been doing in that modest period. Not having a telephone that worked locally, I was going to be highly dependent on the goodwill and co-operation of drivers. Personally I would have chosen to be more tolerant.

Back at UNICEF headquarters, we learnt that we were to be lodged at the Quality Hotel. We collected luggage and I exchanged some US Dollars for a bundle of local currency: grimy, smelly old notes dating from before the civil war. Bernard came with us to make sure the hotel understood the agreed billing arrangements.

The hotel was satisfactory: it reminded me a little of the second to worst one in which I had stayed in Yemen, in terms of its style, basic facilities and décor. It was new, had air conditioning, intermittent internet, and frequent power cuts. The hotel buildings had peachy-pink walls and red-tiled rooves. A single-storey block along the street housed the reception area, and a bar and lounge area, through which one walked to enter the dining room. A two-storey residential block was set further away from the street: the corridor entrances and stair-wells did not have doors, thus blending interior and exterior spaces. All floors were surfaced with ceramic tiles, with varying degrees of neatness and skill, and the same finish extended to the outside spaces which had built-in planters. My room was furnished minimally but adequately; the en-suite bathroom had a shower and the kind of electric water heater I had first encountered in Sana'a.

The reception staff were young, friendly, and very eager to please. Not bad at all, I thought, but Nellie fumed with indignation. She mainly ordered room service meals, and at a point during the weekend, made UNICEF agree to provide her with a car and driver to take her every morning to Lugali House, and then back at night, just using the Quality Hotel as a place to sleep. I made it clear I wanted no such arrangement for myself.

On Friday afternoon we went back to UNICEF for a formal briefing session in the meeting hut, with five members of the UNICEF team. I scribbled a lot of notes. Afterwards, when we were talking informally, Bernard and Simon told me they were Zimbabweans. 'There are a lot of us working in agencies around Africa.' After a pause Bernard explained, 'We are waiting for our President to die', investing those words with depths of resilience and sorrow. As I write this, that was six years ago, and they are still waiting.

On Saturday morning, which was blazingly sunny, we were taken by Charles, Bernard and Simon to the Ministry for a meeting with Mou Mou, the Under Secretary; Shadrach, the Director; and three other senior officials. We parked near to a tree completely covered with flaming vermilion blossoms: I think it must have been a variety of magnolia. We had to check in at a guard house: a routine that became very familiar. The meeting rooms were upstairs in the Ministry building, which was new, pink, and ceramic-tiled – very much in the style of the Quality Hotel. A central quadrangle housed an enormous mango tree. The building must have been erected around it, because it was clearly older: it was the size and girth of a mature elm. Great mangos hung from its upper branches, out of reach.

The meeting was in a conference room: I never got to meet any government officials in their own offices. Mou

Mou and Shadrach were both big strong men with an authoritative manner. Titles like 'Under Secretary' and 'Director' make me think of equivalent junior ministers and senior officials in the UK system, but there is a difference where people have come to power through insurgence and civil war. Looking at those two, I couldn't help wondering about their path to power. How recently, how completely, how permanently, had the use of machine-guns and mortars transitioned into conversations about policy?

They were Anglophiles. Sudan had sometimes been described as 'Africa in one country', with its range of climates, vegetation and landforms, and mix of peoples including the Arabian, Muslim north and Black African, Christian south. Arabic had been imposed as the official language and the medium of instruction in schools: a factor that had reinforced the south's desire for independence. The south's affinities were with Uganda and Kenya. South Sudan intended to be a British East African country. 'English will be the official language and the medium of instruction', Shadrach said, 'And we do mean the Queen's English, not American English or the international Englishes.'

Being driven around Juba, or at least the parts of it to which my business took me, which did not include the town centre, gave me no sense of its urban form. A few main roads probably built in the colonial period had tarmac surfaces and faded white lines and zebra crossings. Most of the roads I was driven on were of red earth. For a populous city, there seemed to be large tracts of very low density development, and great expanses of waste ground, dotted with piles of rubble and strewn with rubbish. Some looked like earthworks for abandoned civil engineering projects; some were protected by wire security fences. Others were populated haphazardly with a few of the round, mud-walled, thatched huts that were obviously the local traditional dwelling. There was also a modern form of these huts, sited, again, somewhat randomly. These were rectangular, probably around a wooden frame, with walls of vertically arranged plant stems like canes or reeds, and with a flat roof covered with a sheet of plastic. By the side of a busy road, there was a patch of ground shaded by a large spreading ash tree, under which people seemed to be engaged in sorting stones into similarly-graded batches, put into containers which had been made by cutting in half the square plastic tanks used to transport liquids. Dozens of these stone-filled containers were grouped as if for sale, although there was no explanatory signage. We passed what must once have been a school, the buildings along the edge of the mud yard battered and derelict: a ghost school.

There were also areas of high-density settlement. I caught glimpses of sites packed with tents. Opposite the Quality Hotel was what I took to be an extensive shanty town, where a proportion of reasonable quality huts was crowded around by a much larger proportion of crude shacks and shelters roofed with plastic and tarpaulins. It had an orderly, settled air, and its own kind of economy: along the road several small kiosks sold things, and chickens pecked about.

I am under-employed: the week-end drags. The smell of wood-smoke is nice; it is the main fuel here. The wildlife I have seen so far includes some big raptors, perhaps blue kites, and a large cicada: you usually only hear them but this one was in a near-death state on the ground; also a grasshopper and small cricket; a lot of unusual moths and a beetle. Large ants invade the corridors and stairwells every night, and the domestic staff sweep them up in the morning. I have managed to photograph a rather plainly coloured lizard which runs along the garden wall, but there is also a more elusive one which is very brightly coloured and likes running up a tree.

The air conditioning is noisy, so I prefer not to use it at night. I wake up thick-headed because of the humidity and inadequate pillow. The room is made up somewhat sporadically, at odd times with no sense of security. It is usual to find that they have left the door and ground floor window unlocked. One day, I saw that the woman was coming to do the room, so I took my book and went to stand in the corridor until she had finished. Afterwards, she said cheerily, 'Why are you standing out here? You don't need to go out of the room for me to clean!' The next day, there was a knock on the door, and, 'May I do your room?' 'Certainly', I said, 'Go right ahead'. Without looking properly, I assumed it was the same person. Too late, I realised my mistake: the room was filled with palpable tension. I sat at the desk, con-centrating deeply on my papers, particularly during the phase of the woman's work that involved her stretching over the bed. Another day, coming back to the room as a servicing woman was coming out, she said, 'You are a good man: clean and tidy'. I didn't think so particularly: certainly I don't have that reputation at home. Passing Nellie's room when the door was ajar, I understood the reason for the comment. It was a pigsty with ashtrays, cigarette ends, room-service leftovers and general untidiness: a housekeeper's nightmare. Thereafter, I became tidier still, making my room look like a barracks ready for inspection.

On Sunday I had meetings in the hotel with Nellie at 13.30, and then with Charles, Simon and Bernard at 14.30. This was to finalise, again, the terms of reference for my project; and to confirm that I would be visiting Rumbek from Wednesday to Friday, while Nellie stayed in Juba.

Monday was occupied by further meetings at the Ministry. My breakfast included porridge; a pancake, sausage and baked beans with what I assumed must be yam – it was white, powdery, surprisingly filling, and sweet; then a small local banana. After the morning meeting, I went back to the hotel for lunch. There was no buffet so I had a satisfactory Western-style meal from the à la carte menu. I asked whether they had tomato juice, assuming it would come out of a carton or bottle. They didn't, but said in a moment of rashness, 'But we can make you one!' With equal rashness, and much against my instincts, I accepted the offer. A long time later, one of the young men came to ask, 'Do you want your tomato juice hot or cold?' Then after a further interval, he reappeared to ask, 'Do you want sugar in your tomato juice?' Eventually a tumbler of mashed up tomatoes was proudly presented to me. There was a television in my room, but I never bothered to switch it on. In the restaurant they had a television tuned to Al Jazeera's English language news channel. I enjoyed its balanced angles on stories; it seemed a lot better than CNN and more interesting than the BBC World Service.

The afternoon meeting at the Ministry was with donor agencies, for whom it was probably fresh ground, but somewhat repetitive for the teams from the Ministry and from UNICEF who were also present, and having much the same conversation for the third time. Charles took my passport and travel permit to see if he could do the necessary registration with the police which was now overdue. That evening I started drafting my report: although most of the fieldwork was still to be done, the general thrust was already clear.

On Tuesday I visited the University of Juba in the morning, and met the heads of the two functioning teacher training institutions in the afternoon. There was not much 'university' to see. The combined effect of the civil war and enforced Arabisation was that the only functioning element of the institution was in Khartoum. What I saw was a small semi-derelict campus, and in a creaking lecture theatre devoid of equipment, I met a handful of staff. They were polite and friendly; some spoke about the work they used to do as if it was ongoing; a few expressed optimistic sentiments. The afternoon meeting was quite different: one of the principals had taken his higher degree at my institution, in the department where I work, so there was more common ground on which to build a professional discussion.

That evening Charles came to the hotel to give me back my passport and travel permit and to brief me for the next day's flight. His attempt to register my presence had been abortive: there had been some trivial problem about payment. The police had to be handed the exact amount of money, and the UNICEF safe hadn't been restocked with the right notes, or something of that kind.

I was excited by the prospect of flying up-country, on what was called the UN food drop flight, although we would not be dropping any food on this occasion. I was to be accompanied by Bernard and Simon from UNICEF, and by Shadrach and Edward from the Ministry. Edward was a senior official whom I had met in several meetings. It would be a small plane, so I could take only a small bag: Nellie agreed to keep custody of the rest of my luggage, which would kipper in the cigarette smoke in her room. The hand baggage rule meant I would need to leave behind my bottles of kaolin and morphine mixture, and J Collis Brown mixture, but fortunately – I felt very pleased with myself about this – I had not yet needed to open either of them. I had with me a business suit, which would stay behind, and an off-white linen suit which would be my fieldwork outfit, with a Tilley hat and a canvas shoulder bag which was just the right size to hold a notebook, a small notepad computer, and a small bottle of water. Charles and others had given me to understand that the hotel in which we would lodge at Rumbek would offer a pleasant experience: 'Oh yes, you'll be OK there', and so, persistently clinging to my illusions I visualised splendid colonial luxury, like Claridges in Delhi, perhaps, or Raffles.

Chapter Twelve

My 'ticket' for the flight to Rumbek was a copy of a brief letter from UNICEF to the Movement Control Officer of the World Food Programme, which did not include a time for the flight. In the event this migrated a few hours from that previously discussed: we boarded at around 13.00. There was a benefit to this delay. 'Oh good', said Bernard, 'We are going on the big plane; we will have a comfortable flight.' The 'big' plane was a twelve seater with two propellers. I had some slight previous flying experience in a very light two-seater plane and in light helicopters; also in the next size up – 20 to 40 seaters. This plane was the happy medium: substantial enough to give a sense of security, while small enough to offer a joyful feeling of flying. It was hard to think that I was being paid for an experience which so thrilled my senses. To complete my bliss, a 'cabin crew' person managed, notwithstanding the cramped space, to offer refreshments, and I received a Styrofoam cup containing hot-ish water and a Lipton's Yellow Label teabag. What could be better than this? Sipping tea whilst sailing between cotton-wool clouds with a motion like gently swelling sea, looking down on African bush – nice 'work' indeed!

The plane flew low enough for me to see every tree and hut clearly, and as we drew near to Rumbek the view became fascinating. For most of the flight, the ground had been the pink of sawn mahogany, lightly freckled with trees. Here and there, straight tree-less pink strips indicated roads. I knew that Rumbek was a significant town in South Sudan: for a period it had been chosen as the intended capital city, until it was agreed that it would be more practical, and less tribally divisive, for Juba to be the capital. So I was interested to see what it would look like. Huts began to appear amongst the trees: they were at first very sparsely scattered, then slightly less sparsely and more evenly distributed, adding a different kind of freckle to the pattern. The tree-freckles continued, unchanged in density or colour, right into the centre of the town. The huts were mainly the tent-sized traditional grass and mud constructions I had seen in Juba. With the addition of the airfield, some rectangular huts of modern construction, and a very few buildings, this was the 'city' of Rumbek from the air.

The airfield was a rectangle of ground enclosed by a wire mesh fence. The earth had been smoothed to make a runway which was an oval, the shape and size of a running track. Some lean-to huts along one side had rooves of blue plastic, and there was a small control tower. I was able to look at these features from a number of angles, because the pilot said he wasn't sure the nose wheel had lowered properly, so we needed to fly round again and pass near to the control tower so they could look at it. We landed smoothly, and walked past a few parked small planes. 'That one is the safest plane: you can come down anywhere', said Bernard, indicating a small plane with perhaps four or six seats, with a fuselage that seemed to be welded onto a sturdy boat hull, in addition to normal wheels under each wing. I saw what he meant: not only would it land on water, but it could swoosh through bushes in situations where a conventional plane would cartwheel. In the terminal hut, the arrivals and departures routes were separated by chicken wire. Outside, young men not wearing any obvious uniform lounged around nursing firearms. We were met by a jeep and taken the short distance to the hotel, driving behind a lorry, to the tailgate of which a man was clinging in an uncomfortable posture.

The hotel was a hutted encampment: a format new to my sheltered experience. We checked in in the administration hut, where a receptionist handed each of us the key to our chalet. The communal facilities included an open-sided barn which was the restaurant, and an amazing bar which was octagonal and built around a great old tree. The trunk ran up through the centre of the building and the branches added to its stability. The frame was made from poles which were tall slender tree trunks from which the bark had been stripped. Joists and floorboards created a ground floor and an open-air first floor, reached by a rickety staircase. The sides of the bar were entirely open to the elements. It was mid-afternoon and after dealing with keys, the receptionist asked whether we wanted something to eat. Breakfast seemed a long time ago so I welcomed this kind offer at least as keenly as the others, and she said she would bring something to the bar. That is where we congregated after finding our chalets, and surprisingly quickly, plates of hot food arrived. Each well-loaded plate included what tasted like smoked fish, although the woman said it had not been smoked, so it may have been sun-dried; a meat stew and rice. We sat at the rough wooden tables talking about the project until sunset. The warm breeze cooled noticeably at dusk.

My chalet, which I thought of as a beach hut, was one of a row of semi-detached units. It was of lightweight modern construction, standing on metal girders raised a foot or two from the ground, with board walls and a corrugated roof. The door was protected by a storm porch over a planked walkway. The interior smelt musty, as if there was a continual battle against mildew. A rag rug adorned the floorboards; the small bed had a thin, almost useless pillow, and a rag-bag of odd coverings. There was a small and very basic en-suite bathroom. The water, from a tank on the roof, was surprisingly icy: there was no functioning water heater. It was a mistake to have left my wind-up torch back in Juba. The hut had a fluorescent tube light that buzzed and flickered faintly for about five minutes before pinging into proper operation: apart from that, I was enveloped in black tropical night.

The next day Bernard, discussing again the attractions of the hotel, said that it was popular with aid agency staff. 'Usually they are living in tents, and the creepy-crawlies come in under the sides, so it is nice for them to come here for a few days.' Luxury is relative: my comparator had been other comfortable hotels, whereas Bernard's had been the old-fashioned UN tents that don't have integral groundsheets. Considering the simplicity of the facilities, it was a pleasant surprise to find that the hotel had wireless internet. The receptionist, or manager, or proprietor, or whoever she was, came to my hut and did things to my small notepad computer, and I was connected. I wrote some e-mails home describing what it was like to be visiting Rumbek.

The hotel grounds included mature trees of various kinds; trees bearing bulbous green fruits I could not identify, and cultivated vegetable plots. Here and there beside the earth paths were additional washing facilities. One was an ordinary domestic wash basin with mixer taps, mounted on a rough breeze-block stand, just sitting there in the open, as one might come across a drinking fountain. Further along was a crude shower, similarly devoid of any privacy. The gardens teemed with wildlife and I wished I had a means to identify birds: by the time I bought *Birds of East Africa* I had forgotten what I had seen. Large exotic butterflies flapped about, near enough to see well.

The restaurant barn was constructed of stripped tree-trunks, a corrugated roof, ceramic tiled floor, and no walls. It was furnished with plastic tables and chairs, and a modern servery. The breakfast buffet offered a fairly basic Western continental range. Tinned pineapple was available at every meal. One of the best elements of the cuisine, available at every meal except breakfast, was dark, cabbage-like greens that were grown in the grounds: I would see staff carrying in baskets of it freshly picked. The meat was disappointingly difficult to eat for one with my feeble Western jaws. Some meat sellers in the UK irritatingly label lumps of beef, carefully cling-filmed to show a lean bit, with vague descriptions such as 'roasting joint' rather than stating properly what cut it is. If you make the mistake of quick-roasting something that actually needed all day, the resultant cross between rubber and leather describes all of the roast meat I encountered in Rumbek. Perhaps it came from older animals; perhaps they didn't see a need to cook it any more – certainly the Africans tucked in willingly. 'Wilkins doesn't eat much meat', opined Shadrach, 'I've been noticing'. It was easier to let him think I was not much of a carnivore than to be candid. Stews were the exception: tall pots of more tender meat with vegetables in spicy, oily soup.

On Thursday morning we set off to visit the buildings which were intended to be the headquarters of the new institute. We had the use of a white UN jeep. Shadrach climbed into the driver's seat with enthusiasm, as if he was back in his preferred element. I sat next to him, and got out my camera, saying, 'I don't have a licence for photography.' 'We are your licence!', he replied. In the area near to the hotel and airfield the roads of packed red earth were broad and straight. We joined a road which could have served as an aeroplane runway which looked as if it went on for ever. There was plenty of spare space: here and there were clusters of round wattle-walled huts. We had to steer around an illegally-felled tree. The men were indignant because it was a mahogany – a protected species.

Under the trees, and set back slightly from the road, were several rectangular enclosures of paling fencing, crowded with huts: the place was more populous than first impressions suggested. I saw people going about their business, parked lorries, the occasional motorbike, and what looked like an Asian mechanised rickshaw. A rather English-looking road-sign warned of humps, and sure enough, the earth surface became so ridged and furrowed, peaked and troughed, that any vehicle without high axles would have run aground. I had been told that many of the roads became impassable during the rainy season.

Shadrach turned off onto a road less straight and less distinct, until we seemed to be just driving through the trees. And yet this was still quite near to the centre of the 'city' of Rumbek: a place where there was no need to choose between a day in the town and a day rambling in the woods. The trees were of various kinds: I noticed that a type of palm tree was common, which held great shaggy fruits, many of which had fallen to the ground. I wondered what it was, and asked if it was a source of oil. No, I was told, it was an edible fruit which was quite pleasant. I looked at the fruit lying all over the ground, and thought of all the tins of imported pineapple rings at the hotel.

The track resurrected itself into a respectable earth road, and a wire mesh fence hove into view, with heavy security gates. We had arrived at the site. Although seemingly in the middle of nowhere, this was an extensive campus of modern single-storey buildings, widely separated by open spaces. These ranged from car parking areas of earth and scalpings, to tracts of rough grass, scrub and scattered trees of many varieties: a campus incorporating African savanna. The buildings had cream-washed walls and low-pitched corrugated rooves which extended to make open external corridors. They included two blocks each arranged around three sides of a quadrangle; an 'L' shaped block and several other buildings. The campus had been the regional headquarters of UNICEF and had hosted some other agencies. It had been gifted to the Government as the base for the new institute and as a temporary headquarters for the planned new University of Rumbek. The site had a skeleton staff – basically a few caretakers – and some residual activity by aid agencies.

Our visit began with a tour of the facilities. There was a space the size of a small school hall, intended for dining and large group events. Rows of empty rooms were designated as lecture rooms, offices and staff rooms, but they were simply empty rooms in a newish building which was already starting to crack and deteriorate. One block contained a suite designated as the Vice Chancellor's office, in which numerous large pieces of new furniture were still wrapped in heavy polythene. At first I was startled by its opulence, as the desk, tall cupboard and other pieces appeared to be of French rococo design, with swirling gilded decorations, and lavish marquetry, inlays and ornamental beading. I looked more closely: it was all made out of plastic.

In addition to the existing buildings, I was told that contracts had been let for the construction of accommodation blocks. We walked through long grass to an older building: a barn-like construction with an open frontage. This was the electrical generating station. It was empty, but our arrival disturbed some game-birds like small grouse. 'We call them wild chickens', Bernard explained. He also pointed out two generators. One stood upright in the grass; the other lay on its side at an odd angle. Bernard explained that the building was not quite tall enough for the generators, and that the attempt to put one inside had resulted in damage to the building and the generator. So there it lay, rusting and inoperable, and no-one mentioned any plan to rectify the matter. By way of compensation, Bernard proudly showed me a neatly planted orchard of young mango trees which were doing well. 'I planted these with my own hands', he said.

A consultation meeting had been organised, accompanied by a light lunch. The five of us were joined by about ten other people. In addition to the few based on site, there were representatives of the regional administration, the university and the diocese, and a regional UN official. I scribbled notes in an A4 exercise book, which when folded in half fitted into my shoulder bag. In Juba, Charles had been discussing the tensions among regions, and between regions and the national state, and to illustrate these he had told me about the hand-over ceremony in which these buildings had passed from UNICEF to the Government, which he had witnessed. It had been a formal occasion, in the presence of representatives of donor governments, including the Japanese and the Dutch. The highlight was the passing of the key to the representative of national government. The representative of the region, in whose territory the buildings stood, thought that he should have it, and at the 'key' moment dashed forward and fought his national colleague for possession. The outcome of this physical tussle, apart from the shock and embarrassment of various parties, was a victory for national government.

That evening, back at the hotel, we talked at length over a leisurely dinner. The Africans were in celebratory mood. For them, the site visit and meeting implied that we were on our way: that the planned developments would happen. My brief required me to build into my report a ridiculously optimistic timeline for the new institute to become operational. Who was kidding whom? The visit also confirmed to me, and I would have to let them down gently on this, that the site was in the wrong place. It was 240 miles from Juba, over earth roads impassable in the rainy season, and not near to any substantial institutions or infrastructures: it would not work as a national headquarters.

Yet sitting in the dark around a communal stew-pot, in good-natured companionship, it was hard not to half-believe that, not necessarily according to plan, but somehow, some day, the project would fly. Launches, celebrations and opening ceremonies seemed much more important than workaday practicalities, and in that spirit they were talking about traditional opening ceremonies. One involved killing a bull, jumping over it, and scattering some blood. They joked that I would have to do this for the new institute.

On Friday morning we checked out and were driven to the airfield for a flight supposedly at 09.00, which would mean 09.30 at the very earliest. The chicken-wire cages were quite busy and the officials became officious when I walked in the wrong direction in order to buy some tea. We waited a long time, much of it out in the blazing sun in order to get away from the congestion. Standing on the red earth, entertained by the aerial acrobatics of some large raptors, getting fed up with waiting, I wondered how it would be if the project developed and I needed to commute here on my own.

What do you do if you are standing in the open waiting for a plane to pick you up, and it doesn't come? On this occasion, deliverance happened after an hour or two.

In Juba, heading into the town, we met a substantial motorcade moving in the other direction. Vehicles of all kinds took up the road space and crowded us onto the rough verge. They stirred up clouds of dust making it hard to see our way. The vehicles were covered with people, hanging out of windows, filling lorries, sitting or standing on roof surfaces. They were in a high state of excitement, shouting and waving their arms. The drivers hooted horns and swerved crazily: just within my own sightline I saw two separate collisions. I asked my companions what was going on. 'A political rally' was all they were prepared to say.

When I got back to the Quality Hotel, I looked into the bar and lounge area. In the unlikely event that Nellie was there, I could have retrieved my luggage. I opened the door a few feet and surveyed the room. The hum of conversation died, and between twenty and thirty black faces turned in my direction, with eyes agog. Only then did I consider how I might look to them. Unlike the hotel staff, these people did not know me. My crumpled cream linen suit, Tilley hat and canvas shoulder bag were smothered with red dust, as were my hands and face, the moreso because I had not washed whilst away from Juba. I would have looked distinctly weary: colleagues tell me so – 'You look shattered', 'You look really ill' – when actually I'm just thinking. To these people, I must have looked like a Brit pretending to be David Livingstone. I retreated and went to reception to sort out my return. The young men on the counter were as friendly and enthusiastic as ever. They were also tending to an African checking in or out or just passing, who wore an ill-fitting suit of brilliant magenta satin, with bright orange shoes, a multi-coloured silk shirt and various vibrant accessories. In my room I enjoyed a long shower, the water running off me looking like mud.

Xavier was in e-mail communication regarding my draft report, as one would expect, but there was another matter on which he made himself a bit of a nuisance. Exposed to Nellie's intensive lobbying, he wanted my recommendations to give greater attention to English language teaching than I considered proportionate within my terms of reference. More significantly, he wanted me to give public assurances that my organisation had agreed to be his bidding partner for an English project when the aid agencies offered funding. My work concerned setting up an institute of education, and even there we would keep future options open until there was actually something real to bid for. I suspected, as proved to be the case, that it would be years before donors and GOSS would be ready to do anything. Xavier said that Mary had given him that assurance during their negotiation of my project: perhaps he believed that but I knew she would not have done. It was not our policy and any decisions about teaching English would involve a different department. 'She's superior to you, isn't she?', Xavier persisted nastily, and started bombarding Mary with e-mails saying that I was breaking agreements and he was not happy, until Mary, despite her exemplary patience and diplomatic balm, finally gave a snappy response. He was way out of his depth for the role he had set himself.

This battle of wills had not yet peaked when I returned to Juba, and Xavier invited me to go to Lugali House to have a discussion with him and Nellie, after which they would entertain me to dinner. 'I'm sure you'll appreciate a pleasant evening here after your trip to Rumbek,' he added unctuously, as if it was the Ritz; as if UNICEF was not covering the costs of our meals. So, shortly after I had showered and changed, I set off for what I suspected would be a waste of time.

I found them in the eating area and we talked across quite an expanse of table. I ordered a cup of tea, which did the hotel credit, being a pleasant Kenyan variety served in a cup the size of a pudding basin. We talked, although neither of them seemed that much interested in the details of my project. Instead, Nellie went on and on about how her project ought to develop into more work for herself, talking mainly to Xavier along what I suspected were pre-arranged lines. I didn't see that it had much to do with me, but they implied I would need to know all this for my report. Disliking manipulation, I took the ground of independence: 'Of course I shall report as I find; my recommendations will reflect the evidence,' I purred unhelpfully.

I was hungry and looked at what was chalked on the blackboard, excusing my interest to the others by saying that I had special dietary requirements. It was a short list of what were definitely bar meals rather than fine dining. A member of staff told me that this was the lunch menu, which was finished with now, and the dinner menu would not be revealed until the right moment came. The discussion continued, with Xavier setting out his position in relation to bidding for future projects, and expressing what was probably genuine confusion about how decisions got taken within my organisation.

At last, with a flourish and sense of occasion, the waiter turned the blackboard over to reveal the dinner menu. It was another slightly different short list of bar meals. Of the two that I might otherwise have considered eating, one was smothered in lemon juice, and the other in cheese, both of which I have to avoid. I made my dietary excuses to my hosts and ordered another cup of tea, and attempted to concentrate on enjoying it while the others had their meals. As soon as I judged it to be permissible to leave without impoliteness, I thanked them for the tea and for the useful discussion. Annoyed and hungry, I intended these words to be imbued with a strand of irony, but they seemed to be taken at face value. Back at the Quality Hotel, I enjoyed my own company and a late dinner in its perfectly adequate restaurant.

Noise woke me up on Saturday morning. The noise clarified itself into a lot of young men chanting whilst running past my window. They wore shirts of a similar colour and looked fit and strong. They were moving in time to their chant, with that distinctly African motion which is a kind of dancing jogging, at a pace which could be maintained. They made quite a noise, and there were a lot of them: perhaps two or three hundred. The scene reminded me of television coverage of events in South Africa, where a group moving and sounding like this would have amongst them a hapless individual with a tyre round his neck, on the way to ritual immolation. There was no such victim today, but the group projected intimidating strength and I was glad to be indoors.

I had business at the UNICEF compound, and during the visit, Charles said, 'There is someone here who wants to meet you.' He left the hut and returned with a young woman, whose name was Rose. A year or so ago she had taken a distance learning course, and I had marked some of her essays. Although I could not recall the work, it was strangely satisfying to have this chance face-to-face meeting with her in such an unlikely setting.

Back at the hotel, people came to see me. One was with one aid agency; a small group was with another. A man came emphasising the confidentiality of the encounter: he had formerly worked with the Ministry. I was intrigued, but the conversation covered nothing significant. The hotel hosted an event on Saturday night which filled it with people shouting at each other and to the world at large, focused on a big outside barbecue. The reception staff told me it was a political meeting. The week-end proceeded into Sunday in tedious under-activity. Like a monk in a cell I tinkered with my report, alternating that with work on the other writing project I had taken with me. Power cuts were frequent. The hotel's internet was not wireless, but depended on a wonky cable that frequently failed half way through an e-mail.

I had arranged with Charles to go to his office at 16.00 to print off some copies of my report to hand round at my presentation the following morning. Through the intermittently available e-mail (my only means of communication) this arrangement was confirmed. I waited in the garden, looking at lizards. After about 20 minutes Charles appeared and drove me to UNICEF headquarters, using a route that involved walking-pace, crazily-swaying progress across deeply potholed earth tracks. In the wooden shack that was his office, he made tea and we chatted generally, including about his research interests. We got down to the business of printing my report, but at quite an early stage the printer made an unpleasant noise and stopped. While Charles fiddled with it, I detected a smell of scorched plastic and some wisps of smoke under the desk. I crawled under to investigate, and said, 'Charles, you have a fire in here!', doing my best to blow out flames consuming some important-looking cables. We discussed extinguishers; he went to fetch a sand bucket which proved effective. I had been concerned that the densely-packed dry wood shacks and thatched rooves could have burned dramatically. Obviously there would be no hard copies: Charles thought that didn't matter because the attendees would be happy with the e-mailed version.

That was a fair assessment. A roomful of interested parties listened to what I had to say and seemed content; a reasonable discussion ensued. Nellie spoke briefly about her own work. She was staying on a few days longer; I went back to the hotel to check out and await pick-up at 14.30. The local authorisation for my stay had never been completed. I had told Charles that I was worried about problems when I tried to leave, and he had assured me I would be accompanied. My driver to the drome was a tall uniformed UN official. After parking, he took my papers from me, and holding them and a great wad of banknotes about two inches thick, led me into the small departures section. There, he talked cheerily to each of the several people present, and distributed the banknotes. Stamps banged onto my papers, and in a few minutes I was ready to go. Getting through into the departure lounge involved a minutely thorough search of my bags and pockets. The 'lounge' was a crowded, stuffy area, its only facility being a Portaloo with no internal light and a dodgy door.

My flight left at 17.45 and afforded some very good views of the Nile – that was the closest to it I was going to get. It arrived in Nairobi at 18.30, where I had some time to kill before my flight to London at 23.45. Hanging around in the terminal at Nairobi felt like a homecoming to Western civilisation. Compared with previous experiences, my body had held up remarkably well to the combinations of stress and food of the last couple of weeks, coming straight after Arabia and China. Now, with the stress over, that false state of well-being disintegrated. I found a toilet, where the sole cubicle (mercifully vacant) offered a raised, throne-like facility. Having produced an effect like an exploding cess-pit I worked on washing my hands thoroughly. The washing area seemed quite large, and I hadn't noticed that I was monopolising the only source of soap, nor that others were present. An Englishman politely alerted me, 'You seem to be scrubbing up to take out someone's appendix – can the rest of us have a turn?'

Chapter Thirteen

The Marriott label adorns hotels spanning a range of quality grades and levels of catering. I am still weighing up the one I have just checked into in Denver. The room is fine, but apart from breakfast, the catering seems not to rise above a few light bar meals, to be taken mainly on high stools in a noisy general area where televisions project American sports programmes. The staff's main language is Spanish: at reception, they rustled up an English-speaking manager to deal with me. Internet connection is $24 a time, so I won't be sending regular news bulletins.

There is an officiousness to some aspects of America. I transferred flights at Minneapolis, and was welcomed with chivvying shouting. 'Did I see you cross that yellow line?' demanded one man, his hand drifting towards his revolver. Before my recent African trip I had decided, somewhat belatedly, that I ought to lock my luggage: a prissiness I soon grew out of. I had bought a kind of combination lock which could also be opened by a key, not provided, but possessed by security officials. A red band popped up to show if it had been opened that way, and it was showing now. Sure enough, when I opened the suitcase there was a card on top, with Spanish writing. Has Spanish become the lingua franca of the USA? The obverse, in English, took about 200 words to explain that my luggage had been gone through.

I am here by my own choice and at my own expense, to present a paper at a massive American conference which takes place every year in April or May. Usually there are about 12,000 delegates and 3,000 contributions: it swamps a town for a few days. I first went to it in 1999 when it was held in Montreal – a rare step beyond the borders of the USA – and then in New Orleans in 2004. Unusually for me, it was actually the conference theme which prompted me to come to Denver. When it was announced last summer it seemed to me to invite a geographical view of education issues. I was once a geography teacher, and my daughter was completing a geography PhD. I thought it might be fun to combine geographical ideas with my current interests; my daughter encouraged me and gave me some modern texts. Our plan was that after Denver I would re-work the paper for the Royal Geographical Society's conference that autumn, when she would be presenting on her thesis, and we could attend each other's papers: all of which transpired very enjoyably.

Meanwhile, this intellectual tourism was a self-indulgent attempt to counter-balance last term's schedule, and to maintain a rounded professional profile – for my own satisfaction, not because I thought anyone else would notice. So I flew out on Thursday 29 April, landing in Denver at 20.34, making the evening well advanced by the time I got to the hotel. The conference starts tomorrow, getting going around the middle of the day.

On Friday morning, Denver was cold and windy. It had a lot of high rise buildings, grid pattern streets, and trams. At first sight the overall conference experience seemed similar to previously, despite my six years' absence. I was given the thick telephone directory style book of sessions. They used to send it, but now it was on-line (if you could be bothered to work out how to browse it, which I didn't), the paper version was given out at registration, so the first task was to sit and plan what to do. One of the friendly Americans on reception, noting where I came from, was much taken with the Englishness of my outfit. Chosen for comfort, it included jacket, waistcoat, tie and cap in the same light blue tweed, and I decided not to explain where Harris is. The conference spanned lots of venues to walk between, and an enormous convention centre. It had whole day scheduling with no meal breaks between 08.30 and early evening. People hurried between venues clutching bananas and snacks. The food available was very expensive. I bought a really plain tuna sandwich which was about £6. Later, snared by its aroma, I splashed out on a hot snack of pulled barbecued pork, with barbecue sauce, in bread, which I gobbled before it got cold whilst perched on a stool in a draughty walkway.

The breakfast buffet had included a great bin of whipped butter, to save the effort of spreading. A fat wobbly couple took piles of it to their table to start the day as they meant to continue. Near to the butter a woman dispensed eggs, which were only available cooked to order – no handy trays of fried and scrambled under lamps. I thought it would be alright to shove a banana into my pocket for later. Someone saw me, and next morning a placard displayed a price for 'fruit to go'. The hotel's evening offering included soup of the day. 'Today's is barley broth: it's really good!' the man on duty exclaimed, seeming genuinely surprised and delighted as if that was rarely the case. I took it as my main course, my only course, and it did indeed represent the high point of eating in Denver. Food seemed scarce. I knew that couldn't really be true: I was just not looking in the right places, but on my routes I seemed not to pass any grocery stores or cafes. I needed tea bags. The hotel included a shop which offered a combination of tourist gifts, many with a Native American theme, and travellers' necessities, among which I found just one packet of one kind of black tea bags which were of very poor quality.

I ambled along the pedestrianised mall of 16th Street to the Civic Centre Park: a massive public open space with the State Capitol building on one side, and the City and County building on the other. Both were in the classical style, and either would have been impressive as the parliamentary building in the capital city of a medium-sized country. But this was America, of course, where everything is calibrated differently. The former looked several times higher than St Paul's, and was topped with a dome covered in gold leaf. Numerous statues graced the park, depicting things of local significance, such as a cowboy on a bucking horse. The sky was steel blue, and trees were only just coming into leaf. I passed rows of yellow school buses. On the return walk, looking north-west, I had good views of distant snow-peaked mountains above the buildings, and with a small frisson realised that I was looking at the Front Range of the Rocky Mountains. That notwithstanding, on the basis of my minimal sampling of the city, and being massively spoilt by London, I felt that Denver was a bit of a one-horse town, a one-day town.

As I appraised and ruminated on the environment and the event, my comparators were my previous attendances at the conferences in Montreal and New Orleans. Memories swirled around. Although eleven years, and a lot of bumpy stretches on life's journey, had passed since I went to Montreal, that trip had special significance. It represented my breaking out of a kind of mental paralysis regarding international travel. I had got into thinking that it was something too difficult for me to do. Partly as a way of dealing with that, I had chosen a programme of doctoral study which included a compulsory international element. As a warm-up exercise, we had a family long week-end in Paris – an immense and memorable achievement – a couple of months before the big thing of my going to Montreal on my own. And it was a big thing: before I used internet or e-mail, the bookings involved letters taken to post offices. Without a courier or companion I had to work out how to board the flight, how to do everything. In Montreal, staying in a much grander Marriott for a whole seven nights, I was beset by unnecessary fears about obtaining cash and paying the final bill, and lived simply, mainly off picnics in my room. I explored early in the mornings, not having adjusted to the time change, and was delighted to see red-winged blackbirds and chipmunks. I made one telephone call home using the hotel phone; and suffered an awful sick headache on the return flight. But the spell was broken, the door pushed open: I could travel on my own. I had also, incidentally, satisfied that unit of my course, by choosing a specialised topic, attending over thirty sessions reporting recent research, and publishing an article about it.

Five years later in New Orleans, I was more confident about travel, and it was good to have been able to see the city before it was damaged by floods. Easter was late that year, so I watched the Easter Day parade in all its Dixie Americanism. I loved the exquisitely ornate balconies of the old French quarter, ate gumbo, drank cocktails and dodged torrential showers. One day I took a stern-wheeled paddle steamer to the east bank. The Mississippi was as wide as the Humber. On the other bank the residences were of wooden construction, stylish in their shapes and colours. I stood for a while by the garden of one, where dozens of Monarch butterflies were zooming about. The Milkweed or Monarch, *Danaus plexippus,* was the first colour plate in the *Observer's Book of Butterflies* which had been one of my boyhood bibles. I'd never seen one, nor seriously hoped to, but now they were flapping around touching my head and hands. On the ferry back, a group of young girls tried experimentally to proposition me: 'Do you want us in a photo? Are you here on your own? Would you like some female company during your stay? What hotel are you in?' And so on. Of course, on the west bank, we went our separate ways.

In Montreal I had been amazed by the conference as a means of learning. Full papers were presented with military efficiency: I went home with a suitcase full of them. In New Orleans I didn't learn quite so much: the themes seemed less clear and many presenters thought PowerPoint was a substitute for writing a paper. In Denver, while I got some useful information for a book I was writing, overall the downward trend prevailed. Some sessions were downright weird. I attended one which took the form of an earth-worshipping, nature-worshipping drama involving men covered in leaves. My session for presentation was on Monday afternoon. I left on Wednesday 5 May on an 11.15 flight to Detroit and thence to London, arriving at 07.40 on Thursday, which meant I was home in time to vote in the General Election.

I also turned my attention back to Saudi Arabia. The hard-negotiated contract was rolling along, with the next week of training happening the following week, but I had decided some time previously that this did not require my presence. That was the right decision: the group sizes were small, no problems arose and the team enjoyed themselves. Meanwhile, Fatima had been busy networking and presented us with a new business development opportunity. This concerned some ambitious plans based on the new King Abdullah Economic City (KAEC) which was being built to the north of Jeddah. The key contact was a senior project managing official called Omar. He invited me to a site visit to find out more, then to submit a proposal. My organisation's senior management were happy to fund the trip and what amounted to free consultancy. Later I found out that two competing organisations had received similar invitations: one Canadian, one American.

Omar issued the invitation letter for the visa but some problem arose which might have meant re-scheduling. So Fatima walked into the Embassy in London, spoke to the right people, and presented me with my visa. I was to fly via Frankfurt to Jeddah on Friday 28 May, lodging in the Hilton, and to meet Fatima there on Saturday morning. The plane took off shortly after 10.00 for the short flight to Frankfurt. When I landed there, it seemed to be a big, busy transfer point, but I found an information screen and checked that my onward flight was on time. Yes, there it was showing at 13.25. Looking at my watch, there seemed to be plenty of time, so I started exploring the terminal.

I passed a café, and thought it might be nice to eat frankfurters in Frankfurt. Service was a little slow, but the light meal was fine: the frankfurters were accompanied with potato salad and dill cucumbers: all very Germanic. Whilst eating, amongst the background noise and not really listening to anything, I half-caught, perhaps a quarter-caught, an announcement for a passenger, of the format one often heard. I ambled along to the gate, and was surprised not to see the usual crowd of passengers: perhaps I was earlier than I thought. I asked the member of staff whether this flight was going to be the 13.25 to Jeddah, and she said I'd better walk straight on. At the top of the gangway, at the moment of stepping in and showing my boarding pass, the person I showed it to seized a microphone and announced 'Boarding complete' and the door slammed shut. I found my seat in the packed cabin and the plane started taxiing immediately. Disorientated by this turn of events, I wondered what had gone wrong. Then I realised: I had relied on my watch, not the terminal clocks, and had forgotten the time difference between London and Frankfurt. How could I have been so careless? What if I had missed the flight?

After landing in Jeddah at about 20.00, I went through the entry procedure and baggage hall, and after collecting my suitcase, there was a further passport check, which was unusual. I fumbled for my papers, and afterwards shoved my passport roughly into a side pocket of my jacket, which was not where it belonged, intending to put it away properly the other side of the doors. Once through the doors, I encountered a particularly assertive offer of a taxi, from a man who had a friend loitering nearby. 'No, it's OK, thanks, I am going to get one of the official taxis', I said, pointing in the direction where they line up, and keeping a tight grip on my luggage for which he kept lunging. 'Yes, that's right, this is for the official taxi', he insisted. I hesitated: perhaps that was the system now, and seeing my resolve weaken, the man took firmer grasp of my case, so that we were walking along both clutching the handle. With reluctance, fearing I might be behaving impolitely, I let go.

The man dashed off ahead, his companion running even faster in front of him. I had to run to keep up. Outside the building, he headed not towards the official taxi rank, but into the darker depths of the car park. Hurrying to keep sight of my case, I had to step over kerbs and barge through bushes. Eventually I caught up with them at the car – large and dark-coloured in the gloom, where my case was already in the open boot, and the back door open to receive me. The man snatched my hand luggage. I remonstrated: I said I wanted an official taxi. 'We are official', he said, showing me some kind of authorisation letter. I asked what fare he was proposing to charge. 'No problem!', he kept saying, waving his hands in the air, all innocence. I kept asking; he kept saying 'No problem!' until I made it clear I was going nowhere until he had stated the fare. Under sufferance, he said, 'It will only be ...' and named a price over double the official fare. Genuinely angry by this time, I shouted 'No!' in Arabic, which surprised him, and in that momentary advantage snatched back my possessions and headed off into the dark, back to the terminal, and an official taxi.

After that irritation, it was very pleasant to enter the familiar comfort of the Jeddah Hilton. Yes, they were expecting me at reception: a room was booked. 'Passport please,' the young man asked routinely. His expression became more quizzical as I confidently groped in my inside pocket but my hand came out empty; I tried the other inside pocket; and, puzzled, pulled out the very full contents of both inside pockets and went through the pile with mounting disbelief and concern. I felt towards some other pockets and found the passport hanging four fifths out of my side pocket, and remembered I had shoved it there. What made me sweat was thinking how easily it could have fallen out during the chase through the dark bushes in the airport car park.

A luxurious bed, a sumptuous breakfast, and Fatima's merry smile contributed to a sense of refreshment on Saturday morning. We rehearsed the plans for the day. Fatima's enthusiasm for the project was partly personal. She had benefited from the King's strategy to modernise his kingdom by educating women at Western universities. She saw the whole KAEC project as a further step towards social reform.

A car sent by Omar collected us. On a map KAEC was just to the north of Jeddah. On the ground this meant an hour's drive through desert. For long stretches of the journey, the views to either side of the road were of flat expanses of very pale yellow sand meeting cerulean blue sky. In places where the sand was higher than the road, it was hummocked into small dunes. Only small areas were vegetated, sparsely, with tough blue-grey tufts of grass and small patches of ground-hugging shrubs. Sporadic human artefacts, all inexplicable to me, included a metal pole here, a few concrete bollards there, serving no obvious purpose.

I was interested to understand the rules about the use of these desert areas: who owned the land, what could other people do on it, how it all worked. I tried asking Fatima but didn't get very far. I don't think she could grasp the question, coming as it did from British notions of different types of land ownership and tenancies, common land, squatters' rights, planning permission and all the rest. She would have had a different set of concepts.

We entered the outskirts of the new town: a massive building site with half-finished roads and skeletons of buildings at various stages. Amongst that overall impression was a tiny proportion of completed and functional buildings, serving a pioneer community and the construction workers. The car drew up at a building that looked as if it was designed to become a mosque. A servant came out and took over from the driver as our chaperon. We followed him into the cool, dim interior, where another servant bearing a tray gave us glasses of red-tinged fruit juice. Always wary of citrus fruit, I tasted it gingerly. It was interestingly pleasant but I couldn't place the flavour, until the servant explained,

'It is cherry juice', which I could not remember experiencing before.

Omar was petit, bearded, bespectacled, softly-spoken, courteous, intelligent and powerful. In his office he explained the project and what it needed from us as the potential partner. He took us into the main body of the building, which was currently set out as an auditorium. Usually an auditorium either has permanent theatre-style seats, or removable chairs which according to the grade of the place range from stackable plastic to fully upholstered. This auditorium went several grades higher: enormous, luxurious settees provided the seating. They were all identical, perhaps five rows of four – something like that – presenting an ocean of richly embroidered fabric. We took our places in the otherwise deserted hall to watch a promotional film about the new town: its port, its university, its attractiveness to international businesses and partner organisations.

Omar took us to a display room shaped like an apse which was lit by large unstained windows with pointed tops. A gigantic oval table bore an architectural model showing how KAEC would look when it was finished: quite like New York from the air would be a fair summary. From the model I could make sense of the complex coastline, with its inlets and islands, which was impossible from ground-level viewing: it was populated with models of the commercial ships and pleasure boats which were intended to flock to the facilities. Omar operated a bank of buttons which illuminated the central business district, the Islamic banking district, the high-class waterside residential area, the educational city, the industrial area, the docks. He explained plans for diversifying industry using plastics derived from oil; plans for efficient use of energy; and plans for education, including the university, a teaching institute, and various schools.

In response to my question he explained that KAEC would be a non-segregated city, operating as an international enclave exempt from the strict religious rules which applied to the rest of the country. I thought of how Hong Kong – this was my analogy not his – had its separate character in the period after it was handed back to China. Here the dual purpose would be to make the place attractive to an international community, and to demonstrate to the rest of the country the advantages of reform. The university had already started functioning: it provided post-graduate study in science and technology. The students were 95% international, and once they had been admitted through the selection process, the courses were free of charge to them. Omar took a series of photographs of Fatima and me standing in various positions by the model, on his camera and mine. These were not tourist mementoes – well, not entirely – but might feature as part of the official story in the event of the partnership project developing.

Next Omar escorted us to the roof, which in the Arabian style had paved walking areas between and around domes. I was startled by the strength of the on-shore breeze. Adjusting to the bright light after the shady interior I spent a while taking in the views in all four directions. In front of me, a park was in completed state; beyond that a sandy site with cranes and piles of materials stretched into the distance, between a natural-looking creek and a man-made harbour. The water in both of these, and in the Red Sea in the distance, was extraordinarily bright azure blue: azure indeed, as if the sea bed was of lapis lazuli rather than white coral. The park in the foreground had lush green lawns laid out in curving patterns, children's play equipment, palm trees, round shelters with neatly thatched rooves, and walkways paved with marble. Beyond the harbour, great blocks of buildings were under construction; between them and the water was what I took to be an esplanade in the making, resting on arches like a railway viaduct. The scenes to the left and behind were similar: green parks, extensive water features, buildings under construction. To my right, the sea came in nearer, to what would become a promenade. Near to where we were standing, a water feature had been made. It was rectangular, dotted and edged with round planters containing palm trees, all of which were bending in the wind. The tiled interior matched the colour of the distant sea. The planters formed convenient perches for some large dark sea-birds which were probably a kind of diver.

Before we left the building it was time for a bathroom visit. In the facility next to the auditorium, the items which would normally be either of porcelain or stainless steel appeared to be gold-plated, and wrought in ornate scallop-shell designs. The taps, mirror-frame and other fittings all glinted in the same high-carat finish. Omar took us to lunch, which involved walking a few hundred yards to a completed section of esplanade. The promenade was paved with red bricks, separated by a low sea wall from the beach a few feet below. Its surface was punctured by lines of palm trees, of a variety which had chunky trunks which looked like pine cones, topped with a cluster of foliage at an acute angle from the vertical, like a feather duster. The building frontage was a row of arches in honey and apricot shades of stone-work. The row included several cafes: outside these, the promenade had been colonised with outside furniture and additional planters. Given the wind and dazzling light I was pleased we were to lunch inside. The place offered practical, workaday catering, mainly in Western style. Omar hospitably ordered prodigious quantities of food: I remember enormous bowls of salad; fruit and vegetable juices; baked potatoes; probably some meat or fish, but mainly I remember a lot left on the table when we had finished.

We were taken to the high-grade residential development and looked round a show apartment. The spacious accommodation included a maid's room as standard. The front windows looked across a band of garden to the waterside, where each apartment had a private mooring. I asked the price – it's nice to get estate agents excited – and it was about the same as the price of a two-bedroom flat in my home area. Next we went to the part of KAEC designated as the 'education city'; we were shown round the multi-purpose building which would be the headquarters of the proposed institute, and met some people. We had a final business discussion regarding how I would write the proposal. Driving back through the desert, Fatima and I were equally enthused by what we had seen: the breadth of vision, the scale of construction, and Omar's quiet confidence that things would happen. The creative challenge of writing the proposal was stimulating in itself, but no project materialised. Civil engineering is so much easier than social and institutional reform, and no-one had reckoned on the impact that global economic problems would have on the hoped-for levels of inward investment in KAEC.

Chapter Fourteen

Gordon and I are sitting in amiable companionship on opposite sides of a formica-topped table in one of the catering facilities in the extensive transit area of Bangkok Suvarnabhum airport. We each have a pint glass: his of cola, mine of tomato juice. 'I've never known anyone drink as much tomato juice as you,' he comments, although in fact it becomes part of my staple diet mainly when I am doing business travel, when alcohol is best avoided. Gordon approvingly lists some technical-sounding bio-chemical ingredients that are apparently doing me good. My main fondness for this stuff is that it is a handy way, given my intolerance of citrus fruit, of counterbalancing the gut-gluing combination of in-flight food and stress.

We have only about half an hour free: our flight on Thai Airways left Heathrow at 21.30 yesterday, which was Friday 9 July 2010, and landed at 15.05. Our connecting flight leaves at 16.05 and lands in Guangzhou at 19.55. We have come to deliver the first China-based element of the contract my organisation won during the

March event. We must perform intensively for four days, starting tomorrow, Sunday, with a new and untested client and partnership arrangements. Our confidence is supported by our experience of team-teaching in Yemen and working together in Riyadh. We have the pleasant anticipation of fellow tourists, used to travelling together, at the beginning of a holiday.

Emma had actively involved herself in the arrangements. The host organisation – a university – had proposed that we stay in the Zhujiang Hotel, but she had done a site check on it and decided we would be more comfortable in the five-star Jianguo Hotel in Linhe Zhong Road: British Council would cover the cost, and she was there in the foyer when we arrived. She sorted the practicalities, and told us about morning pick-up by the university. The university had wanted us to have a briefing meeting with their team of interpreters that evening: Emma had decided we would be tired after our journey and had moved it to the morning. All was well: my holiday frame of mind continued to sail along, helped by a comfortable night and the breakfast buffet being not at all bad. It offered the extensive but slightly odd assortment typical of international grade hotels in China. Each item was of good quality, prettily presented on fancy stands and dishes: a bit of international; a bit of American; bits of various different kinds of Asian, but to get a manly plateful meant assembling a cross-cultural cocktail. I tried a 'salted egg' which looked fairly normal: it was strong and salty, and fortunately nothing like the '1000 year old' variety.

In the foyer we met Joe from the university. He was not a chauffeur: he was the senior manager who had set up our involvement. Joe was tall, bespectacled, obviously able and successful, yet also quite burly with the build and body-language of a night-club bouncer. From the moment of meeting him, Joe oozed an aura of strong-willed authoritarianism, self-confidence and ambition. Nothing subsequently altered those first impressions, although later we both noticed that Joe was also a bit of a loner, who did not seem to mesh very comfortably within the social groups of his organisation.

Sunday morning in Guangzhou was busy and traffic was thick. Joe drove us himself, on a route that crossed the Pearl River. The bridge was approached by an eight-lane highway, which augmented with a series of long slip-roads extended to ten and twelve lanes. These compressed into a mere six for the crossing. The river at this point was wider than the Thames but not as wide as the Humber. Joe's workplace, the campus which was also the venue for our programme, was located a short distance from the bridge on the opposite bank from our hotel. My mind was swirling with what I had to do so I was not paying much attention to the scenery, but Joe pointed out the sights as he drove. 'And on your right, that tower is the most seshewal building in China!' 'I'm sorry?' asked Gordon, raising an eyebrow. 'Seshewal, like a woman body', Joe clarified, giving a foretaste of his sense of professionalism.

Suddenly we were at our destination, turning off the main road into the campus. I had a fleeting impression of an open space surrounded by tall buildings, a lily pond, a parking area, a vestibule, a lift rising to an executive-level floor, then crowds of people all talking at once. The confusion resolved itself into discernible patterns. Determined to be the first to catch my eye, to take control, was a small, mature, formidable woman who was the head of department, flanked by various acolytes. Near at hand, like a cage of fluttering birds, stood the group of interpreters waiting to be introduced and briefed. They were students, or some may have been junior faculty members: young, eager and on trial. I discovered a couple of days later that the ones who performed best would be allowed to accompany the delegation to London. A crowd, variously composed, was flocking around a hot water urn near which was the welcome sight of piles of Lipton's Yellow Label tea bags and paper cups. Emma and a colleague were present from the British Council, and there must have been someone from the provincial government.

Then there were the programme participants: predominantly male, and exuding the opinionated self-confidence that characterises gatherings of school principals worldwide, regardless of race, culture or language. These particular ones had been further inflated by having been told by the Communist Party that they were an elite, selected as the up-and-coming reformers, honoured to be included in this august development activity, which would equip them to lead the province's school system to glorious achievement. My first impression, later confirmed, was that there were a few high fliers, but that the majority were pretty pedestrian. Their image was not helped by their rag-bag outfits of casual shirts with odd jackets and trousers, all very ill-fitting. It was easy to forget how recently the Chinese had been freed from identical Mao boiler suits.

Of course we had prepared a programme that had been approved by all the parties, but it was half way into the afternoon before it settled down to run as planned. Formalities had to be observed: dignitaries had to bless the proceedings in their own time and fashion. I was cued in and made some formal remarks on behalf of my organisation. As the Chinese spoke Chinese, and the help I was getting from one of the interpreters was patchy and scarcely audible, it was hard to know what was going on: what was expected of me. I spoke to politely blank faces; after my diplomatic opening comments I thought I was now cleared to start introducing the programme itself. No, the inscrutable expressions became frissoned: I had jumped the gun, others had to have their say. Other raggednesses became evident. The host university should have spent the previous afternoon briefing the delegates about the UK education system. One of the British Council personnel told me that had not happened: they had used the session in some other way. I guessed the host university would have taken advantage of the opportunity to impress on the participants some messages of their own, which were probably not consistent with or helpful to our programme.

We were taken out to lunch by the host faculty team. This involved a short walk around the corner to an aquarium: that is what the restaurant seemed to be at first sight. We walked through a large covered but open-sided area, with a wet floor and a great many large open glass fish tanks. An impressive array of specimens – some large, some brightly coloured, some weird freaks of nature – swam, writhed, snapped their claws, and tried to look as unappetising as possible so as to prolong their existence. A few paces into a more enclosed area, we came to a round table and sat where we were told. I did my best to make conversation with the people within earshot, but I can't remember learning much about them. Food arrived in the form of numerous small courses. One particularly small dish included what looked like tiny gastropods: de-shelled winkles or snails each the size of a grain of rice. I couldn't think of anything else they might be, but I was puzzled by the mental image of a group of drudges armed with pins, picking them in sufficient quantities to serve up like this.

At a point in the meal, towards the end, and clearly as a highlight, the uncooked head of a large tuna was carried in on a platter, glaring at us in toothy defiance as John the Baptist might have done. Two waitresses carved tiny fragments of fatty flesh from the severed surface, and these were passed round on plates that could have been borrowed from a doll's tea set. It was no hardship that the portion was so small: the flesh was tough, greasy and tasteless. The waitresses carried away the head with alacrity: clearly no question of any second helpings. Dealing with caterers for an event or business meeting in London often involves choosing from one of several grades – of sandwich platter, for example – according to budget and the importance of the guests. I imagined similar negotiations here: perhaps this was the 'B' grade banquet, where the tuna head appeared, but only for three minutes' worth of fragments.

At the end of the afternoon, Joe showed us to a lounge for the use of special visitors, which was to become our base for breaks and the place where we would plan and review with Joe before and after each day's sessions. All of the spaces we used were along the same corridor, which was near the top of the building. The tea urn for general use was in the corridor outside the main teaching room. The visitors' lounge was at the other end. It was furnished with large, soft leather settees, a glass coffee table, a couple of desks and its own hot and chilled water supplies. This luxury contrasted with the only available toilet facilities, which were nearly next door, by the top of the stairs. These seemed to be of student grade: a basic urinal and a row of cubicles with squats, and one tap but no paper, soap or towels. I find it almost impossible to use a squat whilst wearing a business suit, so had to regulate my body accordingly: one of several reasons why it was a relief to get back to the hotel at the end of the day.

Next morning we went with Joe to the visitors' lounge before the start of the session. He wanted us to try various special kinds of green tea, all of which I found mildly unpleasant. He made them by brewing the tea in a quarter-cup of hot water, then adding three-quarters of chilled water. After suffering one or two of these vile tepid offerings, I said that I would really prefer a cup of hot tea. So, using the same variety of dried pondweed, he filled the cup two-thirds with hot water. I reached out my hand in eager expectation, but in his strong-willed manner, he then added the final third from the chilled tap. Joe gave us a few lychees, saying they were particularly good at this time of year: which they were, much better than the UK supermarket variety, so we 'mmm...d' with genuine appreciation. 'I will have some sent to your hotel' he promised.

Joe was keen to provide corporate hospitality in the evenings. We weren't so keen: we had work to do for the next day's activity, and big e-mail in-boxes requiring attention. We valued down-time and private space; we didn't find him particularly easy company. Joe, however, seemed to want to make the most of our presence: perhaps to enhance his status; perhaps to do things he enjoyed under the guise of needing to entertain us. Both Gordon and I might be considered straight-laced: not much given to frivolous entertainment. In the course of discussing various possibilities, Gordon mentioned that he had heard that a foot massage offered a pleasant experience. 'OK, I'll arrange that', Joe had promised.

Packed lunches were brought in for the whole group: we had ours with the faculty members and interpreters in the visitors' lounge, filling up all the easy chairs around the glass table. The lunch came in thin plastic containers, and included a cup of soup that was a stock of meat or poultry, which I found refreshing. It also included a bag of prawn crackers, chopsticks, and the main meal box in which rice was topped with an array of vegetables and bits of meat. The quantity was generous, and the awkwardness of tackling it with chopsticks pretty much filled up the lunch break, when added to my visits to the urn to get proper tea made with properly hot water.

At the end of the day, we lounged in the visitors' lounge with cups of less satisfactory tea while Joe finished doing things in his office along the corridor. He collected us, put us in his car and drove a short distance through busy streets until he stopped outside a grand-looking building. He guided us into a reception area and spoke with the staff in Chinese. We were escorted to a locker-room changing area, where attendants indicated that we were to exchange our clothes for a large towel. I took this unexpected turn of events with only a mild degree of anxiety, braced by memories of recent nude spa experiences. 'Are you OK with this?' Gordon asked me with caring concern, himself opting for the modest method of changing which I associate with childhood beaches.

Wearing our towels, we were escorted along an internal pavement of damp stones to a row of showers. Entering the cubicle I found it to be fitted out to resemble a mountain stream, with bits of rock and fern stuck around the walls. Someone had gone to a lot of bother but the work was crudely done and the overall effect not convincing: it was still a shower cubicle. After showering as perfunctorily as I dared – so as not to get left behind – we were then escorted past a swimming pool, which I was determined to keep out of, and into the stifling oven of a sauna. This was interesting, pleasant, worth coming to. The room was quite large, with a semi-circle of slatted benches facing a roaring fire. Men sat sweltering in groups, covered to the extent of their choice by their towels. Every so often, a man would ladle water onto the fire, causing a sizzling burst of humidity. I liked it for the novel sensation, because it was good practice for enduring tropical heat, and because I pretended to myself that this would massively cleanse and benefit my skin. I would willingly have stayed longer, but the others were ready to go, so I followed them back the way we had come. Apparently it was necessary to have another shower. Another token visit to the mountain stream; another reminder of a classic advertisement for mentholated cigarettes. Then we returned to the locker-room, to exchange the towels not for our clothes, but for a pair of embroidered silk pyjamas. 'Whatever next?' I wondered, stoically doing my duty, earning my crust, avoiding diplomatic ructions. The outfit comprised a sort of blouse and short trousers with baggy, flapping legs. It felt cool, insubstantial, and inappropriate for a business meeting. The locker-room attendant was over-attentive, fussily valeting. Later, on the way out, he seriously thought I would appreciate help putting my knickers on.

Joe led us along a corridor, up flights of stairs, and into a self-service buffet restaurant. The food was far-eastern but not Chinese: Korean or Thai, perhaps. I filled my bowl, joined the others at a functional, wooden canteen-style table, and fumbled with the dainty, shiny chopsticks. Who seriously thinks these are suitable for picking up and eating whole French beans covered in slippery oil? After the meal, and tea, Joe guided us to an area where ranks of towel-covered loungers were arranged in front of a large television screen showing an incomprehensible and uninteresting Chinese programme. We settled into three vacant loungers in a row. 'I want you to feel very relaxed' was Joe's irritating justification for the ensuing period of tedium. Fortunately this was not prolonged. An attendant came and whispered discreetly in Joe's ear, whereupon he roused us and guided us up some more stairs in what was obviously an extensive building. We came to a dimly-lit corridor housing a row of treatment rooms. Three doors were open, and three masseuses smilingly greeted us. After all that hanging around and showering, it was good to know that at last this was where I was going to get my feet massaged.

During the next day, the third day of the programme, I became aware of a certain about of restlessness among the participants, and some shifty expressions on the faces of members of the host faculty. The participants did not like carrying out group-based learning tasks: a problem I had encountered in my first Chinese workshop in Beijing. 'We've done that, we've finished' they would say: anything to get back into the more comfortable setting of listening to a lecture. Regarding the members of faculty, I hadn't known they were going to be there, and had no idea what they were actually saying when they sat with and interacted with groups of participants. Pre-course liaison had not included any opportunity for us to brief the host team or to explain the teaching and learning methods we were using.

This was symptomatic of a wider issue. The project involved five parties: the provincial education department, my organisation, the host university, the British Council, and the course participants. Each party had read the same description of the project, but had elaborated and visualised their expectations in their own way. And each party, ourselves included, had to some extent assumed that the other four parties could read their minds.

By now I had had time to look properly at the campus. My spot for reflective pondering was the window near the tea urn, which looked down onto a shorter building and a running track. The shorter building, of about seven storeys, was finished in pink and white horizontal stripes. It stood beside a full-sized running track surfaced in the same shade of pink, with a grassed central area. Beyond were rows of five-storey residential blocks. From my viewpoint, all the spaces between and around these buildings were filled with the Hooker's

Green crowns of trees, vigorously thriving. I remembered that this damp luxuriance of growth in a crowded city centre had been a marked feature of my previous visit to Guangzhou. At ground level, coming out of the block where we worked, was the row of spaces where senior staff parked their cars, with the lily pond beyond, and one of several student accommodation blocks to the left. Much washing was hung or strewn across the balconies of the latter, giving the impression of a tatty tenement, although the grade of the building was not bad.

The lily pond was my favourite feature: I gave it my attention as we walked past. It was a large rectangle, heavily populated with several kinds of water plants: regular water lilies with floating leaves; a variety of lily that poked its leaves well above the water level, and a more rugged plant with leaves like wild rhubarb. The pond was edged by trees, and in the far corner was a small pagoda-like ornamental structure. Just to its left, in the middle distance framed by tower blocks, rose the Gangzhou Tower to which Joe had so excitedly alluded.

The last day of the programme was quite burdensome, because we had to check out of the hotel, take our luggage to the university, organise a full day's activity including hearing the participants' group presentations, and, in my case, last out without using a proper toilet until we reached the drome for our evening flight. The participants' presentations were astonishingly awful. The groups had not engaged with the set task and had lacked the skills to work as a team. Each spokesperson, instead of reporting their group's activity, simply ranted on about the merits of what they did in their own school. No wonder they had been bored by the task. I gave frank feedback, and to give them their due, when the participants came to London in September they had all transformed their approach.

The day was also quite taxing on account of how we had been spending the previous evening. Sitting in the capacious chairs in the visitors' lounge at the end of the previous day's session, Joe had explained that we would be guests of honour at a dinner with the Vice Chancellor that evening. 'He likes to drink white wine with dinner, are you OK about that?' White wine seemed harmless enough: I said that would be fine. 'Oh good', Joe replied, 'A lot of Britishers find white wine too strong!' Really? Not the Britishers I know.

After interminable hanging around and more cups of luke-warm pond-water, it was time to go to dinner. We were shown into a private dining room with a round table with a central turn-table. While silk-clad staff fussed over details, we paid homage to our host, and to his lesser (but still vastly important) acolytes – Deans of this and that. Tiny tasting-sized portions of red wine were poured into miniature wine glasses, posing the problem for people used to knocking it back of how to drink this politely – pretend it is Communion? Meanwhile the Vice Chancellor was getting excited: 'You must have some white wine!' Far from producing white wine, servants poured out some kind of spirit from a container like a pretty porcelain oil drum, and a glass was thrust into my hand. Our host's order, 'bottoms up!' had to be obeyed. The spirit was of at least vodka strength and had a slightly maizey, malty flavour. So this was the 'white wine'. Food appeared;

the turntable turned, the meal proceeded, punctuated by thimbles of red wine and glasses of spirit. As a special honour, we had to drink a delicacy. This time things were floating in the spirit: long white filaments of something. 'White wine with fish sperm!', our host announced. 'Bottoms up!'

The meal proceeded merrily, with Sino-British relations being much advanced. Toasts were proposed. After a few of these, Gordon nudged me helpfully: 'I think you had better propose a toast', so I dutifully toasted the University, its Faculty of Education, and the ever-prospering partnership between our institutions. I was aware of becoming slightly tipsy; aware also that we had work to do and tomorrow's lessons to prepare. I remembered long ago seeing the television coverage of Richard Nixon's visit to China, in the days when he was still taken seriously, and how he raised the glass to his lips, taking only small sips. That was probably connected with his downfall. More toasts followed, to whoever or whatever came into people's heads. I tried the Nixon trick, but was spotted straight away, committing this sin against the good relations between our countries. The Vice Chancellor proposed a toast to somebody important and said directly to me, 'And for this I must insist on bottoms up!'

Gordon knows medical stuff. When we sat down, he said 'Don't worry, our livers are stronger than theirs.' I found this reassuring and it turned out to be true. Over the next hour, our good British livers, evolved over generations to cope with being steeped in Pusser's Navy Rum, London Dry Gin and Scotch Whisky, kept us on the right side of stupidity. By then, our hosts were shrieking with hilarity, falling off their chairs and thoroughly enjoying themselves. We parted the best of friends.

A driver took us back to our hotel and we agreed that tomorrow would get sorted out tomorrow. In my room I was greeted by a substantial crate parked in the middle of the carpet. The outside of the box was covered in printed images in a garish oriental style. Against a dazzling lime green background, fat Chinese characters were coloured rainbow-fashion in shades graduating through puce, purple, turquoise, lime and lemon. On one of the sides of the box was a similarly garish picture: of lychees. With a sinking heart, I prised it open. It was full of tree branches with leaves, and among the leaves, fresh lychees. Hundreds of them. Joe had been as good as his word. What on earth did he think we could do with so many lychees? I ate a dozen or two before giving up for the night. The next morning I gave Gordon the few branches he would accept, stuffed an unwise number myself, and hoped the hotel staff would have the judgement to steal the rest.

www.ingramcontent.com/pod-product-compliance
Lightning Source LLC
Chambersburg PA
CBHW051414090426
42737CB00014B/2669